The Raw Truth

A Pimp Daughter's Diary

Dr. Venus Opal Reese

Copyright © 2019 Dr. Venus Opal Reese
All rights reserved. No part of this book may be used or reproduced in any manner whatsoever without prior written consent of the authors, except as provided by the United States of America copyright law.

Published by Best Seller Publishing®, Pasadena, CA
Best Seller Publishing® is a registered trademark
Printed in the United States of America.
ISBN 9781712638569

This publication is designed to provide accurate and authoritative information with regard to the subject matter covered. It is sold with the understanding that the publisher is not engaged in rendering legal, accounting, or other professional advice. If legal advice or other expert assistance is required, the services of a competent professional should be sought. The opinions expressed by the authors in this book are not endorsed by Best Seller Publishing® and are the sole responsibility of the author rendering the opinion.

For more information, please write:
Best Seller Publishing®
1346 Walnut Street, #205
Pasadena, CA 91106
or call 1(626) 765 9750
Toll Free: 1(844) 850-3500
Visit us online at: www.BestSellerPublishing.org

FREE GIFT!

https://venusopal.com/gift/

Learn the logic of how I became a millionaire & join The TRUTH Tribe!

Praise for Dr. Venus

"Dr. Venus is an unstoppable speaking force that any group or individual would be blessed to experience."

"Dr. Venus shows up, turns it out, and moves a room in a profound way. As a 21st century thought leader, she pulls inspiration and commitment from the depth of her being and touches every heart, soul, and mind in her path. Dr. Venus is an unstoppable speaking force that any group or individual would be blessed to experience."

Suzanne Evans
Chief Movement Maker

"You must experience Dr. Venus Opal Reese!"
"I couldn't hold back my tears of joy and triumph—she is so extraordinary and powerful."

Kym Yancey,
Co-Founder & President, eWomenNetwork

"Dr. Venus is nothing short of a modern-day Prophet."

There is no other messenger like her when it comes to tellin' it like it is in a way that calls people up to confront the lies that hold them hostage. Her words are like a heat-seeking missile, cracking open her audiences and her clients. As a mentor and friend, I have had a front-row seat to her always-unfolding purpose-driven life, and so should you!

Lisa Cherney
Host of Get F***ing Real Podcast
www.GFR.life

"Venus is a walking miracle who cares about helping others."

She has been able to turn her tough background into success. From the moment you hear Venus speak, you can feel the passion she has for changing lives. She is the real deal.

Larry Benet,
CEO and Co-Founder of SANG

"Like lightning in a bottle."

"Impactful and bright. In a word, unforgettable."

Andrea J. Lee,
Founder, Power of Coaching LIVE

"Dr. Venus is a Master Trainer who actually delivers. Her incredible insight, wisdom, and brilliance make her one of the best and brightest in Black America today."

"I am picky. It normally takes a speaker up to 3-5 years to get on the PowerNetworking stage. Dr. Venus did it in three months. This sister knows what she is talking about, and she consistently produces incredible results. She is serious about empowering our people economically, not simply motivationally. Dr. Venus is a master trainer who actually delivers, which is why I invited her back to my stage and made her part of my faculty."

George C. Fraser,
CEO, FraserNet, Inc.

"Dr. Venus Opal Reese Rocked My World FROM THE MOMENT I MET HER!"

Her passion for helping others is apparent, and her presentation for my audience was filled with rich and relevant content you can put into practice right away. I have no doubt many lives will be transformed by Venus' amazing story and step-by-step system.

Michele DeKinder-Smith,
Founder and CEO Jane Out of the Box, Inc.

"Dr. Venus...has taken the pain of her past and turned it into HUGE profits!"

"I consider Dr. Venus the 'Queen of Self-Esteem.' Coming from humble beginnings, she has taken the pain of her past and turned it into HUGE profits. I've had the privilege of watching her produce unprecedented results over and over again. This woman knows how to make it happen in a big and impressive way!"

Lisa Sasevich,
"The Queen of Sales Conversion"
The Invisible Close

Offerings

Prologue	2
Uterus	8
Unleashed	13
Tomorrow	17
Body	19
Dragon Tattoo	22
Hope	27
Transaction	30
Atonement	36
Protection	42
Maybe	46
Fire	49
Gangsta	52
Hate	60
Addiction	67
Stand	74
Covered	80
Artist	84
Pimp	89
Musings	100
Baby	110
Even	114
Joy	122
War	130
Home	138
Guilt	144

Dedication

To all of us who still bear the scars...

...and to those who love us back to life.

We thank you.

Ps: God is so faithful.
Thank you for never leaving me.

Prologue

When a woman speaks her truth, she breathes fire.
A fire that burns down the lies
scorches through façades and
lights up the dark nights living in her soul.

When a woman speaks her truth
she bitch-slaps shame, regret, and self-sacrifice.

Her tongue becomes a flame.
Her voice, gasoline.

She spits truth like red-hot embers burning down
generations of making it work,
making do, and overcoming.

When a woman speaks her truth,
it serves as alchemy, revealing the
charlatans in her life. Her truth burns
them to a crisp.

Truth. Is. Fire.

It purifies.
It refines.
It shapes.
It destroys.
It illuminates.

*And just like fire, truth can be turned up or down.
The difference between a campfire and a forest fire is
rage. It can keep you warm, or it can ravage all the
strongholds you hold as truths.*

*They are not truths.
They are bondage.*

*Taming you.
Containing you.*

*Shackling us to other people's approval.
Other people's
agendas.
Other people's gods.*

*White women roar—it's heard as power.
Black women breathe fire—it's heard as anger.*

*Truth is fire.
It is audacious.
It is bold.
It is unapologetic.*

*The truth will set you free, but
first, it will annihilate the house
of cards you call your life.*

*When a woman tells her truth,
she is a fire-breathing dragon.
Soaring about the mayhem of her life
pouring lick after lick of burning hot
flames on to the illusion she called
happiness.*

*My life had to burn to the ground
so I could find me again.*

*Create me anew.
From ash to clay.
From clay to dirt.
From dirt to I Am.*

*When my life imploded
I folded in onto myself.
I cocooned.
I thought I would emerge a beautiful butterfly.*

I was wrong.

*I came back as myself.
My full self.
My whole self.
My authentic self.*

I came back a dragon.

Now, I breathe fire.

Let me help you be brave...

Every person has pain, and every woman has a walk. I have walked through life's fire and bear the scars.

I went from living on the mean streets of Baltimore to Stanford Ph.D. to multiple seven-figure earner. (Hold up. Let me stop right there. No, not about the money. No, the education part.)

Don't let the Stanford Ph.D. fool you.
I am more street than Stanford. #realtalk
I am not nice.
I am not politically correct.
I am not neat.
I can't promise you perfection.
I can promise you my truth.
I am a hot mess on a good day. #youthinkimplayin
Sometimes I curse, I cry, and I pray—in the same sentence.
To say I am edgy is an understatement.
It would be more accurate to say I am raw.

Raw words.
Raw feelings.
Raw e.m.o.t.i.o.n.

I am sharing my world through words with you. I am a bunch of other people when I speak. I am most myself when I dance. I am most honest when I write.

So I am writing.
I am writing about my self-hate for being born. *(My mother wanted to abort me, but my father threatened her life if she did—long story. We will get into that later...)*
I am writing myself into existence as my own resurrection.
I am my own messiah.

So before we start, I need you to know a few things about me, so you can consciously choose if you are brave enough to want me in your ear.

I talk much shit—as an art.

I am multilingual. I speak fluent Street, impeccable #blackgirlmagic, conversational feminism, and can read through bullshit on energetic braille.

I go in and out of vernaculars—from Queer culture to Southern Baptist Church; from academia to hip-hop's dopeness; from spirituality to some gangsta shit—I flow in and out of worlds. And I am comfortable in them all.

So don't expect me to be linear or additive. I create in circles, not in hierarchies. I suck at grammar and syntax. So my participles may dangle. Let them. I did it on purpose.

I break up typography on a regular. And I speak primarily in first person singular even when I'm talking to third person plural. So for all grammatical purists—fuck you.

You should also know that I have PTSD, anxiety, I am dyslectic and am a super high-functioning autistic. I come from a lineage of addicts, street gangstas, and mental cray-cray. I qualify as handicap due to childhood trauma. Some days, getting out of bed is a challenge. Thank God for Happy. He is my puppy. He is my joy—and he insists I get up each day. He is an emotional support service animal, and he helps me cope. I share this with you, so you don't get sloppy. People make judgments because they don't have enough information to make an informed choice. I have been through some thangs, and it will be reflected in my writing.

I have a following on social media platforms of over 100K. I have one rule there, and I will bring it to my writing world: no judging. I identify as Queer. If you don't know what Queer Identity is, look it up. So don't say some bullshit about Trans or Gay people. I will come for you, raw.

Don't say some bullshit about Black Women—I will fuckin' cut you.

And don't say ANYTHING about my relationship with God. I will get on a plane, come to your workplace, and bitch-slap you in front of your boss. THAT'S how hard God and I roll.

Ignore at your own risk.

Whew! Now that I have scared away all the folks who are easily provoked, here is a piece of gentle wisdom to help you walk with me.

It would serve you to read my Word with an open mind. Or don't read it.

Just put the book down. Save yourself from being upset, insulted, offended, or shocked. I am bound to do all of the above.

But if you can let be me myself, my imperfect, wounded healer self, you will expand and heal in ways you didn't know you needed until you read me.

So I invite you,
if you are willing to be brave…

…walk with me.

Uterus

(Just Sharing)

I can feel myself getting quiet on the inside...
Resolved.
Resolute.

Last year this time, I had a procedure done to reduce the size of a benign fibroid tumor in my uterus.

It didn't take.

The tumor is the size of a grapefruit, and I can see it protruding from my tummy when I lie on my back.

The pain of my menses has escalated. So much so, I am on the floor in tears. My doctor had to call in a prescription.

I am choosing to have the tumor and my uterus removed from my body.

I don't want to wait until my body is so pissed with me she has to have me in the hospital because I didn't listen to her.

I'm good with the laparoscopic surgery. I am acting early, so, prayerfully, the surgeon can go through my belly button. I am vetting referrals now so we can schedule the surgery for the first quarter 2019.

What shook me to my core was confronting that I will never have children. Once my uterus is gone, the dream/fantasy/hope expires.

Right now, I am tending to the impact of the absence of my father. It is profound. I find it compelling that my uterus removal is in the same energetic space as me taking on making energetic space for my father to know he is loved. This is the same man who fought for me to be born. And I will never have children.

Walk with me...

I was so afraid I would act out the violence I was born into, I was afraid to have a child. I feared I would hurt a child the way I was hurt. My heart couldn't run the risk.

I have had chances to get pregnant. I have loved both men and women. So it was an option I turned down when I was younger.

As I mature, I face my mortality.

I do not have a legacy.
And once my uterus is removed, that quiet hope in the background of my heart dies.

I am clear I can adopt. I know. That's not this.
I am crystal clear my work is my legacy. That's not this.
I know I can get a surrogate to carry. I will retain my eggs. That's not the rub.

I will never feel life growing inside of me.

And for some reason, there is a loss I cannot speak.

I could try to have a baby. My doctor discussed this option with me. I am 47. It's risky. I would need to start now. If the baby and I made it through birth, the baby might not be healthy. These are all worst-case scenarios, and I am sure I could get another opinion.

That's not my point.

My doctor suggested we could buy more time by taking bioidentical hormones that could slow down the growth of the tumor but wouldn't diminish the tumor. I could keep my uterus. Other fibroids may grow. Or not. We don't know, but all is not lost. There are options.

That's not my concern.

My body has been hurt in ways too vivid for this platform.
I am clear men and women have acted out their wounds on my body.
I know I haven't done anything wrong. I know I am not being punished by God on any level.

All this I know.

I am choosing to have the hysterectomy to claim my body as my own. In a lot of ways, I have spent my entire adult life in recovery.

I have spent my life in reaction.

I have been undoing the damage done and redeeming that which was taken, stolen, or sold to the highest bidder.

No.
Not now.
Not anymore.
I am choosing me.

This is my body.

It is the only one I will have. I get to love it the way I love God.

I never doubt God, so I will not doubt my body. If it wasn't time, it would not be showing up.

I am not what happened to my body.

AND I get to take care of the temple that God has blessed me with until I transition to the next life.

There is no fear in me. Just a destinal resolve to live free.
Free from the past.
Free from the historical wounds.
Free from the hurt acted out on my body that is now showing up in my uterus.
In my body, there are memories that are not my own. Pains and hurts I was born into…

But just because I was born into them, doesn't mean they get to stay in my body.

I get to love this body.
I get to care for this body.
I get to enjoy this body.
I get to live a free life—not suppressed or afraid.

So I redeem me.
I take back my body.
I heal, and I walk in this world, a free woman.
I cannot be contained.
I wonder…

…what will it be like for the world to deal with a free, empowered, limitless, walk-in-my-own-authority, out of the box, ruthless, shameless, unapologetic, educated, whole, rich, accountable, responsible, fearless, truth-speaking, shit-talking, God-loving, gives zero fucks, transformed, healed me?

I feel sorry for the world on the other side of this season in my evolution. I sincerely do.

Thanks for bearing witness.

12/24/18

Unleashed

(I'm ready...) I choose me. I choose to walk in my own authority and let the world bow down.

I refuse to walk in fear.
The devil can't hold me.
I am beautiful.
I am courageous.
I am a free woman.
Loved. Adored. Respected. Admired.

It's time to come out of hiding. To stand in the sun, unapologetically and afraid.

Life is too short to settle. To be unhappy just to keep the peace.
No more.

I think I tried SO hard to NOT be like Momma, people think I'm a punk ass.

Mistaken my kindness as weakness.
My grace as meekness.
My mercy as insecurity.

That's unfortunate.

I'm embracing ALL of me. Including the Momma in me.

Momma gave no fucks. She NEVER backed down, even when she was dead wrong. She played to not simply win but to annihilate.

I thought when I started to cocoon, I would emerge as a beautiful, gentle butterfly. Fragile. Delicate. Lovely.

I was wrong.

When I emerge from cocooning, I'm not coming as a butterfly.

Naw, brah...

I'm emerging as a dragon.

One that breathes fire for breakfast and welcomes the sunset with hot flames as its breath. Fire that scorches and purifies. Fire ruins the old and creates the soil of the new.

What's more: dragons don't fight. They don't squabble over petty shit. A dragon commands.

Its presence is enough.
I am enough. I choose me.
Each morning I thank God for giving me one more day.

As I watch God move through my life and literally burning down EVERY attachment I have held on to (i.e., house, car, marriage, hair, body, business, friends, health, cursing, being Black, being a millionaire, family—all of it) I realize I don't need ANY OF IT. I don't need people or approval or property. I don't need anything that no longer serves my destiny. I. Have. Me.

And that's enough.
I'm more than enough.
I am perfect just the way I am.

It's time for me to live MY LIFE—free from other people's manipulation, guilt, and greed. I'm not responsible for anyone but me.

I'm done with playing defense in hopes of honoring others whose actions have let me know they don't give a fuck about me. That I am only a wallet.

I am a person.
I am an individual expression of God.

Others' jealousy is not mine to carry.
Others' insecurities are not mine to heal.
Others' entitlement is not mine to tolerate.

I am one with God.
I am covered.
I am anointed.

It only gets better from here!

I realize now the most powerful way to fight is to not fight at all.

Stand. And let go. Let go of EVERYTHING I have ever identified with my sense of self. Let. It. Die.

So I'm letting Momma out.
I'm unleashing my inner dragon.
I'm burning shit the fuck down.

Because in the end, when the smoke clears...

...I will be standing on my own two feet, free and unencumbered by the past.

Unstoppable.
Clear.
Breathing fire.

And so it is.

So be it.

Ase

1/24/19

Tomorrow

(I was doing so well...)

I got the call from my doctor today. I need to have my hysterectomy next week. There are two tumors in the walls of my uterus, and they are messing with my kidneys. I will be out of pocket for four weeks.

I feel trapped.
EVERYTHING is on hold.
I feel powerless.

I just went back to bed, ate delivery, and now I want to cry, but I can't.
I wish Happy was home.
I don't have any requests.
I feel despondent. Disheartened. Dejected.

I don't want to do shit. I just want to... I don't know anymore...

I feel hateful right now. I had JUST gotten back to feeling good about me. I was creating the future. Now I have to cancel trips, take myself out of programs, and I ate white rice tonight. I haven't eaten white rice in months.

Gluten, dairy, sugar, and salt don't work for my body anymore. But I didn't care. I ordered in because I couldn't face going outside.
I couldn't face life.

Not today.

I may go get Happy tomorrow, so I am not alone in this...

Nanna is coming.

I told her to wait until tomorrow to confirm that the surgery is going to be on 2/13. The doctor's admin is running the insurance to get everything in order. It will clear tomorrow.

I just feel really low right now.

Please don't tell me to be strong. Or God's got it. I'm not strong, and I know God's got it. I can't hear it right now. Any pleasantries will land in my ear like gravel.

All I can hear is the harsh silence of waiting.

If I were still drinking, I would get fucked up tonight.
When I was younger, I would hurt myself.
Take to the streets and do some bullshit that I knew would hurt me.
I didn't care.
No one gave a fuck about me, so why should I?

I was doing so well...

I could feel my confidence and power restored. Clarity was present. I was creating the future. My future. Now everything is fuzzy. My mouth knows the right words to say. But right now, I can't hear God. I can't hear the whispers...
I felt like an artist again. I was taking care of me. Now I don't care. I just want my puppy.

I have no request.
I am going to surrender the day.
I will try again tomorrow.

Yeah. I will try again tomorrow...

2/5/19

Body

(In my feelings) I've been lying in bed for 90 minutes, trying to decide to lie here and weep or get up and exercise.

My surgery is on Wednesday.

I feel a little achy—when I stress, my body aches.

I ate a shitload of sugar this weekend. Well, a shit ton for me... I had pancakes three times...

I thought about getting Happy and bringing him home today. But I will not be able to walk him for a minute, and he is with other dogs AND learning his commands.

A friend came over last night, cleaned my tub, and straightened up for Nanna. I've given up on folding my clean clothes. Fuck it. I'll just pull what I need from the laundry basket.

I stayed in bed all day yesterday. I can feel my energy seep away through my pores onto the bedsheets.

Perhaps this is my body's way of preparing for my hysterectomy.

I can feel me going numb. Not caring about anything. Dissociating my "self" from my body.

I learned decades ago to separate my self from my body. With every extension cord whelp, water hose whip, broomstick bruise, broken rib, swollen lip, blackened eye, concussion, gun—at my temple, in my mouth, pointed at my chest—every contact high, every Long Island

Iced Tea, Hennessy mixed with Coke, beer cans as weapons, broken bottles as blades, fingers as ropes squeezing my neck, etc., my body was a liability.

Because it could be hurt.

So I turned my back on my body. I gave her to the wolves. Perhaps this surgery is my body's way of punishing me.

It's now two hours later, and I don't know if I should stay in bed or go exercise. I still don't know. Nanna will be here this evening. I will be up by then.

I guess I have made my decision.

I think I will stay in bed.

Lie here and listen to my body. I think she is pissed off with me and has some shit to say. So I will listen. And perhaps...

...maybe...

...if I sit still for a minute...

...and I don't tune her out...

...if I give myself permission to hear her—from Momma's pain to Daddy's absence; from the streets to Stanford; from Defy Impossible to divorcing; from self-mutilation to radical self-care, and from quiet systemic self-hate to soul-stirring self-love...

...maybe, just maybe...

...my body would forgive me?

I don't know.

We will see...

2/11/19

Real & Raw Series
Dragon Tattoo

A year and some change ago, I prayed a prayer. "God, please get what's ever in the way OUT of the way so I can fulfill my destiny."

I never thought it would be my marriage.
I never imagined it could be my body.
I NEVER dreamed it should be embracing my self-hate.

Let me start over.

Actually, let me start at the beginning. My conception.

"Thus saith the Lord, thy redeemer, and he that formed thee from the womb, I am the Lord that maketh all things…"

So God gave me to Momma and Daddy.

Momma loved Daddy.
Daddy used Momma.
Momma becomes pregnant.
Daddy is proud.
Momma schedules an abortion.
Daddy threatens Momma's life if she kills me.
Momma goes to jail for Daddy.
Daddy's warrant won't let him visit.
Momma's love for Daddy turns to hate.
Daddy waits for Momma's release.
Momma gets out of jail because I'm living in her belly.
Daddy comes to the hospital proud.
Momma says he will NEVER see his daughter.
Daddy tries to reason.

Momma picks up the phone to call in the warrant.
Daddy leaves.
Momma becomes a sadist—in the name of love.

"I should have flushed you down the toilet when I had the chance," Momma hurls at me on a regular.
"You ain't shit. Just like your father."
"You are ugly, stupid, and dumb. You should never have been born."
"I hate you. You make me sick. I can't stand you. Get the fuck out my sight! You stupid bitch. Ugly whore. You are good for NOTHING."
"I dare you to cry! If I see one tear, I'll beat the shit out of you! Go ahead and try me! Cry, bitch, cry. I dare you."
"Get on your knees. Apologize bitch for making me hit you. You brought it on your damn self."
"Take off your clothes. Go sit in the tub. Turn the hot water on. I don't want to hear SHIT from you!"
"You are a piece of shit. Always have been, always will be."
"Who the HELL do you think you are??? Give me your money—I been taking care of you all this time. You need to help out around here!"
"Momma loves you. You need to pay the light bill if you want to stay here. At least you are good for something. You need to pay the phone bill next week or get the fuck out!"

I have known my entire life I should never have been born. I was trained from the first day I drew my first breath—I was a breech baby and was blamed for that as well.

Because I knew I should never have been born, I have spent my entire life finding ways to be useful. Paying bills, tending to people who said they loved me, self-sacrificing and acquiescing so I didn't get aborted, kicked out, or turned out.

So when I prayed my prayer to God about my destiny, EVERY structure, relationship, ideal, belief, and stronghold came tumbling down...

...until all that was left was... me...

...me letting go of EVERYTHING I thought I had to hold be loved. My body, my marriage, my hair, my friends who didn't give a fuck about me. My loyalty wouldn't let me see it. I have punished myself for wanting ANYTHING for myself. I don't deserve free air.

It feels like God took away EVERYTHING that I was dependent on. So I am learning that I MATTER as much as the people I call my own. Now that I am on bed rest for who knows how long, I am giving myself the gift of truth-telling. Just for me. I have protected so many with my silence. No more.

I have NO idea what my destiny is anymore.

I don't know what it looks like, and I don't know who I would need to become to manifest God's will as my life.

I am clear as the day is long of what it's NOT.

I don't want anything from this life.
I do want to move to San Diego.
I do want an eight pack of abs.
I don't want to self-sacrifice.
I do want to be at peace with sleeping alone.
I don't want to manage anything.
I do want to explore erotica.
I don't want to be responsible for another human being.
I do want to enjoy my puppy, Happy.
I do want a Harley—or a BMW.

I do want a photoshoot JUST for my dragon! (YAY)
I do want my sales team to outdo me.
I think I want to be a thought leader.
I think I want to be a fitness model.
I do want friends who live near me.
I want a new life.

I am thinking of dropping "Dr." and just calling myself "Venus Opal." It feels like a different person to me. I don't feel the need to say "doctor" anymore. I don't feel the need to say "Stanford" or "millionaire" or "multiple-seven-figure earner."

None of that is me now.

In truth, I don't know who I am anymore. I'm not disturbed by this unknowing.

I am not attached to being rich or poor. I have been both, and neither is better than the other.

I have canceled 2019. No tours. No events. My body will be healing and adapting to the hysterectomy for a year or two. This was very disheartening when I was told. But in truth, my body doesn't have the stamina for the rigors of touring nationally or producing a big event.

I feel like God is MAKING me focus on me totally and completely. And perhaps that's my destiny. Perhaps my destiny is to love me completely as nothing, as a nobody, as a piece of shit. As a girl embryo whose momma didn't want her and whose daddy left her to the wolves.

"Dear God, please get whatever is in the way out of the way so I can fulfill my destiny" was the prayer I prayed that imploded my very existence. In the rubble and smoke, standing in a heap of violence, broken promises, and other people's agendas…

...is a naked little brown girl with terrified eyes and a hunched back waiting for the next blow from life, hugging herself.

I can imagine her coarse hair matted with knots because it hasn't been combed since she was born. No shoes. Callused feet from walking on hot coals to get to a place called Love. I see her hugging herself and saying in a small trembling voice, "I love you, Venus. I love you. I love you. I love you. I love you. I love you. I love you. I love you, Punchy. I love you. I love you. I love you. I love you, Opal. I love you. I love you. I love you. I love you so much. We don't need no clothes or shoes.

I love you. I love you. I love you. We don't need anything they took away. I love you. I love you.
i.
love.
you.

you.you.you.you.you.you.you.you.you.you.you.
youyouyouyouyouyouyouyouyouyouyouyouyouyouyouyouyouyou
youyouyouareeeeeeeeeeeeeeeeeeeeeeeeeeeeeeeeeeeeeeeeeeeeeee
eeeeeeeeeeeeeeeeeeeeeeeeeeeeeeeeeeeeeeeeeeeeeeeeeeeeeeeeee
eeeeeeeeeeeeeeeeee enough.

And she holds me as we walk into my destiny naked to the world... wearing nothing but...

...a dragon tattoo.

2/17/19

Hope

Right at this moment, everything hurts.

My body.
My bones.
The space where my uterus used to live inside of me.

My head aches.
My heart aches.
My soul aches.

Breathing feels like drinking shards of glass and spitting up streams of blood.

Don't fuck with me right now.

Never judge people by how they grieve.
Never judge a person by how they cope.

I need to call my uncle.

My uncle was the closest thing to a father I have ever had.

He took me in when Momma tried to kill me.

Years later, on the other side of three degrees and a Stanford Ph.D., I asked him why he helped me. He said, "Venus, I could see you one day having your own car and apartment. Your mother is crazy. Life made sure of that. You did nothing wrong. I love you."

My uncle's only daughter died too young.
He saw one of his sons shot right in front of his eyes.
When his oldest sister died, he floated away.

He drinks to cope.
He drinks as he grieves.
He drinks to numb the pain.

If I were with him right now, I would buy him the next round.
And the next.
And the next.

Until the pain was pickled, and then we would see what happens...

NEVER judge people by how they grieve.
Never judge a person by how they cope.

I come from a bloodline of addicts, gangstas, and rage.

My people are street. We are fucked up in ways that defy language.
And we love each other. We take care of each other.

We hurt each other.
We hurt ourselves.
I understand why we hurt.
I understand how we grieve.
I understand what we cannot say.

So I grieve on this page.
I bleed on this page.
This pen is my needle, this ink my heroin—taking the pain away...
for a while...

I cope by writing what was never, has never, will ever be voiced.
Right now, everything about me hurts.
But I don't mind.
My momma hurt.
My daddy hurt.
We hurt.
We feel.
We try.

And in between the searing pain required to stay alive...
and the dead numbness of giving up...
...there is a space
a tiny space...

like the distance between
your inhale and
exhale...

...is hope.

vor

2/28/19

Real & Raw Series
Transaction

WARNING: SEXUAL VIOLENCE BELOW.
Do not read this is if you have not healed all sexual traumas you have experienced, witnessed, or participated in. This post WILL trigger you. It will reactivate you. It will send you into a tizzy. #realtalk
For your own well-being, DO NOT READ THIS—EVER!!!!

WARNING: SUBVERSIVE CHRISTIANITY BELOW.
If you're a devout Christian and have a traditional relationship with God, the Bible, Jesus, and the Holy Spirit—DO NOT READ THIS POST!!! It will offend you, insult you, piss you off, and/or make you want to start spewing Bible verses at me as well as defend your interpretation of the Bible. I have a personal relationship with God. I have read the Bible multiple times and know it better than most devout Christians.

So I say this in love and with deep respect: Don't fuck with me nor my relationship to and with God.

It's a private thang and not up for discussion, debate, or correction/criticism. I may be wrong. Or right. That's not my point. My point is this: God has been with me since the beginning of time. You are not my God—so please don't come for me. I will annihilate you if you try. I promise. #myfathersdaughter #protectingyoufromme

~~~~~~

There is a transactional component to even the most sacred things.

Jesus.
Childhood innocence.
Sex.

As a child of the streets, I learned early that EVERYTHING costs. You have to pay to play.

When I was six, I wanted to play jacks. So I gave my first blowjob to my stepbrother, who was in his teens. He played with me.

Here's the truth: It was my idea. And I liked it.

Not every sex act is violent.

Incest. Molestation. Assault. Rape.
Each act has its own hue, timbre, and tone.

Everything for me, especially romantic relationships, love, is a transaction.

Transaction: (n) An exchange, trade, or transfer of goods, services, or funds.

Love is transactional. It can be bought or sold for a price. The price doesn't have to be money. I have bought love with my mouth, my silence, my body, my brain, and my blood.

~~~~~~~~~~~~~~~~~~~~~~~~~~~~~~~~~~~~~~~

I could never buy into Jesus.
I cannot see a man dying for me.
I know—in my bones—you give to get.
I wonder if my father had been around, would I believe Jesus loves me.

Men say they love you, just like Jesus said he loves me. I believe my father loved me. That's why he stopped Momma from aborting me. But he left. He left me to the streets.

~~~~~~

When I was on the streets in my early teens, I was running in circles filled with men three times my age who were into minors. One dude groomed me for him over time.

There is a process of being turned out.

It doesn't happen overnight. It's a seduction of sorts. Instead of flowers and wine, pedophiles court with clothes, a warm place to sleep, and lollypops. Their biggest seduction tools are praise, attention, and love.

A body can be trained just like a mind can. Stimulus. Response. Catch. Release. Push away. Pull back in. Blame. Forgive. Put out. Take back in. Inflict pain. Provide pleasure. Scream. Whisper. Defend. Betray. Turn cruel. Be kind. Threaten. Protect.

I was trained well.

One day Ol' Dude took me by my hand upstairs to his closet.

I was on my period and couldn't perform. (Some men do not like period sex; some men do. Women are different. They can work with it or work around it, depending on the woman.)

Ol' Dude felt tricked because I didn't tell him before we went upstairs. He was right. I know the rules. The streets have a code. Laws. I know not to go upstairs if I am not ready to put out.

But he looked at me like I was pretty. He talked pretty to me. I felt special. He held my hand as we went upstairs.

He held me in place by my throat while he whispered in my ear how he loved me and how my young pussy needed him. He told me how good he would make me feel and how my body was saying something different than my gasping breath.

My body was responding. I was aroused.
His fingers turned to coils as my body ached and arched. I wanted him to fuck me.

He choked me until I passed out.

Violence arouses me. It has since I played jacks when I was a six-year-old child.

~~~~~~

I am not innocent.
Innocence is a function of shelter. Protection. Safety.
My daddy kept me alive, but he didn't keep me safe.
Safety is negotiated. Provision is conditional. Conditions require payment of some kind.

Transaction.

Some of us (whores, bitches, sluts) understand that transaction is code for power.

Power costs. It can be bought or sold with innocence, paper, and even tears.

~~~~~~

I wonder if Mary Magdalene ever thought about giving Jesus a blowjob.

She got on her knees. She was in position.
She used her tears to wash his feet.
She dried them with her hair.
She lubricated his feet with expensive oil.

Jesus was pleased.

When she got on her knees, that's when the transaction started. She knew EXACTLY what to do to get what she wanted from the Messiah.

And it worked.

She didn't need to fuck Jesus to control him. Influence. Sway.

She got on her knees.
She knew *exactly* what to do to get Jesus to trust her.
To love her.
To make Jesus her bitch.
When she got on her knees in front of all the men in the room and treated him like the Son of God, Jesus was seduced. She paid him respect. He paid her with loyalty, protection, and status.

Mary was the first person to see the empty tomb and the first to see Jesus after his Resurrection. Not his boys. Not his momma.

His whore.

And he loved her.
Just as she was.

I wonder if my father knew me, would he love me just as I am?
I am not innocent.
I am not pure.
I am his seed. The one he kept alive but never fought for.

He left like Jesus wept.

And I paid the price.

I doubt if a man could ever love me.
My daddy loved me but left me to a world of wolves where you either pay or die.

I wonder...

...what would I have to pay my father to make him love me enough to stay?

vor

3/3/19

Atonement

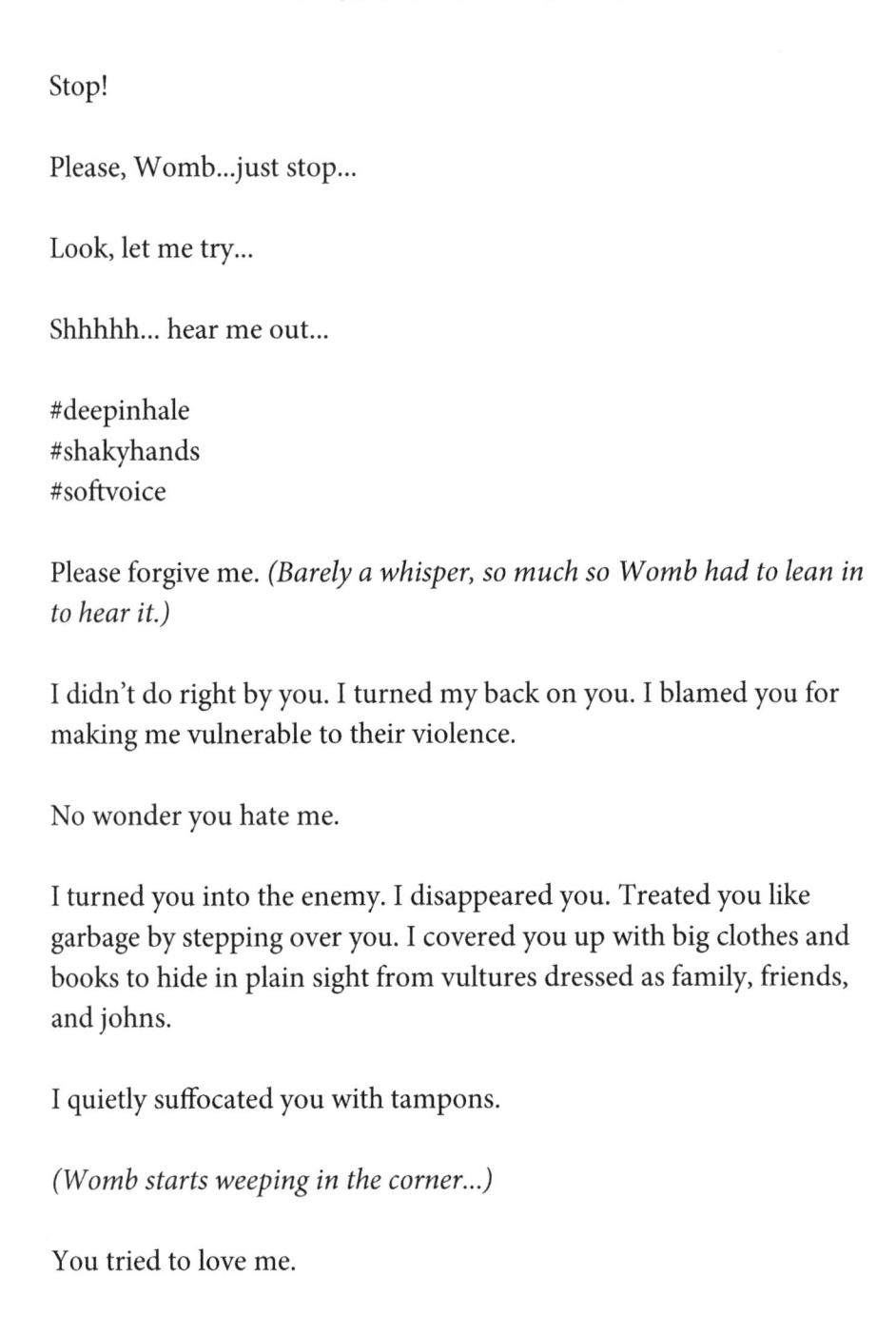

Stop!

Please, Womb...just stop...

Look, let me try...

Shhhhh... hear me out...

#deepinhale
#shakyhands
#softvoice

Please forgive me. *(Barely a whisper, so much so Womb had to lean in to hear it.)*

I didn't do right by you. I turned my back on you. I blamed you for making me vulnerable to their violence.

No wonder you hate me.

I turned you into the enemy. I disappeared you. Treated you like garbage by stepping over you. I covered you up with big clothes and books to hide in plain sight from vultures dressed as family, friends, and johns.

I quietly suffocated you with tampons.

(Womb starts weeping in the corner...)

You tried to love me.

You spat out each unwanted seed from men who tried to get me pregnant for their own agendas—be it a visa from Africa to America or to "set your little ass down" brothers who realized I was more man than they could ever be.

I tolerated you.
I ignored you.
I resented you.

So, of course, you were heartbroken.
Of course, you got sick.
Of course, you developed tumors.

When I rejected you, I broke your heart.

And you NEEDED me to feel pain. Pain like I had caused you. Pain so lightning raw, it would get my attention and wake me up.

I couldn't get off the floor.
Bleeding through my jeans.
Fetal-position pain.

You had to hurt me, so I could feel how much I had hurt you with cold neglect since I was six.

Womb, baby, I am so sorry.
I turned my back on you.
I am sorry I made you leave me.
I hurt you so badly when you left me, you took Uterus with you.
(Remorse seeping from pores.)

I want you to know I know I did this. *(Womb looks up from the corner. Tear-stained face and eyes filled with death.)*

You did nothing wrong, baby. *(Atonement walks slowly, gently toward Womb.)*
It was me.
All me.

(Atonement is standing right in front of Womb. Atonement kneels down, so Womb doesn't have to look up. Atonement starts to speak in a shaky whisper that is riddled with guilt and regret. Atonement starts speaking slowly but becomes more desperate.)

I know I can never get you back, and Uterus is gone too. I know the price I will have to pay for the rest of my life is that we will never have a child.

(Womb starts to weep again. Her sobs shake the very fabric of her soul, and Atonement wants to reach for her, comfort her, but knows it's too soon. So Atonement keeps talking, speaking right to the wound that's as raw as a third-degree burn that hurts when the wind carelessly touches it.)

I know that is what you wanted most of all. That's what you were born to do. To give.

(Womb is sobbing uncontrollably. Atonement keeps going, piercing the boil so it can drain... heals...)

And I took that from you.

(Womb slaps Atonement hard across the face. She beats, hits, scratches, and screams at Atonement. Atonement doesn't defend himself. He doesn't fight back. He just holds her and strokes her hair and back while whispering in her ear...)

I know...
I know...
I am so sorry...

(They sit in silence. Atonement holding Womb. Cradling her. Seconds become minutes. Minutes turn into eons. They sit in this shape, clinging to each other until they are cold.)

I need you to hear me, Womb, please, baby, listen, and hear me.

I. Love. You.

(Womb looks at Atonement with tragic eyes. Atonement bears it all. He tells the truth.)

And if you will let me, I will fill you with a love you never could imagine.

(Atonement speaks truth. Gently. Tenderly.)

I know the price you paid for loving me is irreplaceable, but please, baby, please.

(Womb starts to pull away.)

No, no, don't go. I don't want anything from you.
I want to give you something.

(Womb looks Atonement in the eyes.)

My heart.

Let my heart fill you, Womb.

Let my love saturate every crevice and nook of you until you don't remember the loss...

The Raw Truth

Let me bathe you in tenderness.
Let me caress you with kindness.
Let me tend to you with a preciousness that only newborns know...

(Womb untangles her limbs from Atonement and walks to the window and looks out. Daybreak. It's been a long night. Atonement comes up softly behind Womb and wraps his arms around her waist and whispers into her ear as he presses his body into hers...)

Let me lead you into the light, so you are warmed by the Sun.

Let me take you dancing so the world can marvel at your beauty, while I watch from the sidelines and smile.

(Atonement gently turns Womb around, so they are facing. He gets down on his knees.)

I guess what I am trying to say—ask—is, will you forgive me?
Will you take me back?
I can't replace Uterus or our unborn child.

(Womb starts to tear up again...)

What I can do... *(Atonement takes Womb's hands and holds on to them reverently)* ...is love you and make you my world.

I can give you all the love I should have given you all these years...

(Begging) Please, I know I don't have the right to ask, but please, Womb, baby... please save my life.

(Silence.)

Give me a reason to live. To keep going...

I'm sorry I'm so selfish, Womb. But I need you. I need you to let me love you. Let me make this, make us, right. I want us to be whole. No empty spaces on the inside...

(Womb's eyes start to resituate. Life is starting to seep back into her pores...)

Take me back.
Please, baby.

I promise you, with everything I am, you will be cherished until the day I die.

(Atonement is weeping, tears free-flowing down cheeks onto their entwined figures as if baptizing their love from sorrow and grief.)

So will you? Will you take me back? Will you forgive me?

(Womb stands there, like warm marble. All but her eyes... life is arising in her eyes. Atonement doesn't see her eyes through his guilt and grief yet...)

Baby,
Please...
Please...
Please...

Protection

Where I come from, men are useful.
They pay for stuff.
They watch out for you.
They introduce you to new things.

People.

Places.
Highs.

On the streets, having a man kept a girl-child safe.

(sort of...)

Some men hurt.
But a lot of men helped.

Ol' Boy was a man who helped.

Ol' Boy was kind.

I met him on Chase Street when I was staying with my uncle's ex and my oldest sister. They were close in age. Mid-20s. I was 17ish.

Ol' Boy was beautiful. Hazel eyes. High yellow. 6' 2". Built like a hefty football player you did not want to be tackled by.

Ol' Boy came over with the crew to play spades. His friend was dating my sister, and they all got along great. I was a bookworm, sleeping on my pallet in the front room while they drank, smoked, bagged weed, and talked shit in the kitchen.

Ol' Boy had jokes.

He understood Momma's violence and called her "killer." It was funny. Somehow Ol' Boy made all the bad stuff seem funny.

Ol' Boy watched out for me. When he got a chicken box, he would get me a chicken box. When he went to the corner store to get individual cigarettes, he would pick up a big bag of salt and vinegar potato chips for me. Over time, I started to look forward to Ol' Boy coming through. I knew I would eat if Ol' Boy came by.

I stopped going to school to scrub floors so I could contribute to the rent. There was not a demand to do so. But I felt I would be put out if I didn't do something that they needed. I wanted a stable place to stay, so I figured if I could help out with the bills, they would keep me.

When Ol' Boy saw me at home during school hours, he asked me why.

I told him I needed to bring in money. He listened to my logic and got quiet. Then he said, "I'll trade you. I'll work, and you go to school." I didn't know what he wanted. And it wasn't bad scraping the wax off of the floor and buffing it. It beat being out there—even if I had to give the "guardian" a cut for cashing my check and l let him hold me as he listened to old R&B.

So I kept working.

Ol' Boy bought me food.
He hung around me more and put the word on the street that I was his girlfriend, so no one would mess with me.

He brought me ice cream and would give me unwanted contact highs by blowing smoke in my face from his mouth. But he would never let me get high, and he made sure the other guys didn't slip me a Mickey.

We became good friends.

One night, Ol' Boy and I were walking the block and heard shots too close to be misunderstood.

Ol' Boy grabbed me and forced both of us to the cold concrete that smelled like piss and Mad Dog 20/20. His body was covering mine.

Someone—a young brother—had been shot across the street from us.

Ol' Boy got up and pulled me to the left side of his body on the sidewalk. I tried to look, but Ol' Boy gently said, "No, Venus. I don't want you to remember this."

Then he put his body in my line of vision so I could not see death as the blood painted the concrete crimson red.

After that, I went back to school and made up ten months of work in three weeks.

Ol' Boy gave me money.
He paid for my bus passes.
He brought me clothes.
He provided for me.
He protected me.
Even from myself.

And he never asked for payment.

Ol' Boy would sleep on the floor with me.
He would spoon me, both of us nude, without ever taking liberties.
I offered. I wanted to pay him back for being so kind to me.

He kissed me softly and, with a smile said, "I'll wait."
I didn't understand.
"Is there something wrong with me?"
I was getting nervous.

He just smiled and said to me, "You don't love me yet. I'll wait until you love me."

vor

3/6/19

(Life after Hysterectomy)
Maybe

I think I am done.

I am tired of trying.

Tired of holding it all together.

Tired of cleaning up other people's messes.

I wonder what it would feel like to just quit.
Walk away and leave it all.

What if freedom was letting it all fall the fuck down?

What if I just gave my ex half and walked away to start anew?
What if I closed down my company and went back to teaching? Or consulting? Or nothing at all?

What if I started to date men again?
Just to see if any one of them would truly love me—fatherless, worth nothing, and wombless. I can't give a man a child, so why would he bother?

Without my womb, I am worthless to men.
Without my wallet, I am worthless to women.

What if I didn't owe God shit?

My life has been shit.
I am a piece of shit.
Momma said I would amount to nothing.

Maybe she is right...

Maybe Momma has always been right... What if I stopped fighting to live? Stop proving I have a right to be alive?

I used to fantasize about dying.

The thoughts would dance and swirl around my psyche like sirens. They floated in and out of my imaginings, like freshly fallen snowflakes gently tumbling through the air as an option whenever life tried to kill me.

Thoughts of death were the norm for me.

The only thing that stopped me was Nanna.

I couldn't stand the idea of her finding me in a tub of red.

I have known death.
I have known pain.
I have known loss too titanic to comprehend.
I have known betrayal.
I have known being used.

I don't cry for none of them.

The only thing that makes me cry is kindness.
Nanna is kind, and I cannot hurt her.

But I can hurt me.

Fuck life.

Maybe I will just walk away from it all...

Scrape my dirty flesh with the jagged edge of a clay jar.

Maybe I will lay down this body...
Lay down this willful act of defiance called my
life...
Lay down...

Maybe I will stay down and let everything I have built crash all around me.

Then maybe... just maybe...

I will be free?

3/13/19

(REPOST) I took this down last night because not many people read it. I am reposting it because I forgot—I am writing for me, not you. I will not forget again.

~~~~~~

Real & Raw Series

Fire

When a woman speaks her truth, she breathes fire.

A fire that burns down the lies
scorches through façades and
lights up the dark nights living in her soul.

When a woman speaks her truth
she bitch-slaps shame, regret, and self-sacrifice.

Her tongue becomes a flame.
Her voice, gasoline.

She spits truth like red-hot embers burning down
generations of making it work,
making do, and overcoming.

When a woman speaks her truth,
it serves as alchemy, revealing the charlatans
in her life. Her truth burns them to a crisp.

Truth. Is. Fire.

It purifies.
It refines.
It shapes.
It destroys.
It illuminates.

And just like fire, the truth can be turned up or down. The difference between a campfire and a forest fire is rage. It can keep you warm, or it can ravage all the strongholds You hold as truths.

They are not truths.
They are bondage.

Taming you.
Containing you.

Shackling us to other people's approval.
Other people's agendas.
Other people's gods.

White women roar—it's heard as power.
Black women breathe fire—it's heard as anger.

Truth is fire.

It is audacious.
It is bold.
It is unapologetic.

The truth will set you free,
but first, it will annihilate the
house of cards you call your life.

When a woman tells her truth,
she is a fire-breathing dragon
soaring about the mayhem of her life and
pouring lick after lick of burning hot
flames on to the illusion she called happiness.

My life had to burn to the ground,
so I could find me again.
Create me anew.

From ash to clay.
From clay to dirt.
From dirt to I Am.

When my life imploded
I folded in onto myself.
I cocooned.
I thought I would emerge a beautiful butterfly.

I was wrong.

I came back as myself.
My full self.
My whole self.
My authentic self.

I came back a dragon.

Now, I breathe fire.

Real & Raw Series
Gangsta

WARNING: SUBVERSIVE CHRISTIANITY BELOW.

If you're a devout Christian and have a traditional relationship with God, the Bible, Jesus, and the Holy Spirit—DO NOT READ THIS POST!!! It will offend you, insult you, piss you off, and/or make you want to start spewing Bible verses at me. Or it will compel you to defend your interpretation of the Bible. I have a personal relationship with God. It's a private thang and not up for discussion, debate, or correction/criticism.

I may be wrong. Or right. That's not my point. My point is this: My God is a gangsta.

~~~~~~~~~~~~~~~~~~~~~~~~~~~~~~~~~~~~~~~

Me: *(Resolved knock)* God, are you available?

God: *(Slight pause)* Yes, Beloved.

Me: *(Entering the plush office)* We need to talk.

God: *(Smile in voice)* Of course we do, Beloved.

Me: *(Agitation barely suppressed)* Stop calling me that.

God: *(Soft chuckle)* Oh, you hot, huh?

Me: *(Overtly angry)* Don't fuck with me, Lord.

God: *(Softly, provocatively)* And why not? I'm God. You're mine. And there ain't shit you can do about it. You belong to me.

Me: *(Mad. Feeling cornered)* Fuck you, nigga.

God: Beloved *(God raises a hand sporting the purest diamond in he history of the world, encased in gold, on his pinky finger.)* Bae— I know you are pissed. Do you really want to talk, or do you want to fight?

Me: *(Leave it to God to cut right to the heart of the matter. Through clenched teeth)* Fight.

God: So be it, Bae. What's good?

Me: *(Hip to the game)* Naw, Son—I need some rules. You're temperamental as fuck, Jehovah. And I don't want no shit from you if I piss you off—

God: *(Interrupts)* You can't piss me off—

Me: *(Incredulous)* What the fuck! Lot's wife pissed you off, and you turned her into table salt!

God: *(Sitting back)* That was a misunderstanding—on her part—

Me: You got pissed with the Israelites for doing some bullshit, and you left them wandering in the wilderness for 40 fuckin' years, 20 feet away from the Promised Land—

God: *(Getting a little defensive)* They brought that on their damn selves—

Me: *(On a roll now)* God, you got SO mad at the human race you killed EVERYTHING ON THE PLANET except Noah's family and the two by two—

God: *(Flexing)* ENOUGH! *(Lightning flashes, thunder rolls, and the galaxies hold their breath.)*

Me: *(Calming down but just as incriminating)* You're a fuckin' gangsta, God. So as an Ol' G, I need some rules in place, so you don't come for me or mine—Old Testament style. I know you keep your promises, and your words can never come back void. So I need you to respect my rules.

God: *(Ol' G settles down. The galaxies exhale.)* Fair enough. What are your "rules?"

Me: *(Earnestly)* Just one: that you remember you love me and that you created me in your image. Which means I am JUST LIKE MY DADDY! And remember, I am your favorite. So you can't punish me no matter what I say. Agreed?

God: *(God smiles at his favorite daughter. So much like him, it's almost terrifying.)* Agreed. You have my word. Blood oath Word. So, what's on your mind, Bae?

Me: *(She relaxes and takes a moment. It took eons to get the courage to confront Ol' G face to face. Raw, angry, and desperate)* Jehovah Nissi—what the fuck do you want from me?

God: *(Ol' G sits back in his oversized leather chair that swivels as he reaches into a beautiful mahogany box. He lifts the lid. In it are the most exquisite Cuban cigars in the universe. God fingers the cigars as if they were priceless jewels until his fingers find the one that pleases him.*

He picks it up and slowly rolls it between his forefinger and his thumb. He eyes his creation. The one he created the entire universe for. He marvels at how perfect she is—all fury and righteous indignation. He smells his cigar, bites the tip off with otherworldly perfect teeth, and lights the end with an angel-made pearl lighter. He looks AMAZING in his three-piece zoot suit—pearly white, of course—replete with a wide-brim fedora and gold-handled walking cane.)

God: That's an easy question, Bae. I want EVERYTHING from you.

Me: But how, Jireh? When you have taken EVERYTHING from me?

God: Careful. I didn't "take" everything from you. I simply answered your prayer. "God, please get whatever is in the way out of the way so I can fulfill my destiny." Did you not?

Me: *(Checked. Head bowed.)* I did.

God: So what are you bitching for? I answered your prayer, but because you don't like HOW I answered it, you want to come for me? *(Sigh. Headshake)* Humans. Never satisfied.

Me: Ralpha, I know I prayed that prayer, but I never expected you to Job me! You took EVERYTHING—my marriage, my health, my confidence, my ability to have a child. You took my worth, friends, my ability to make money—everything.

God: *(On some God shit.)* Yes. I did. (*Turns to his right and his enforcer is right there to do his savage bidding.)* Gabriel, pour me a snifter of cognac, will you? Thanks. *(Gabriel does his bidding.)*

The Raw Truth

Me: I don't know who I am anymore. I used to be so sure of my purpose. Jesus had a purpose that was crystal clear. Fuck Jesus. You ALWAYS loved him more than me. Yet you murdered Jesus but kept me alive. Why? What do you want from me?

God: *(He listens deeply.)* I already told you. I want everything from you. I. Want. You.

Me: *(Perplexed)* But Jireh, you already had me?

God: *(Jealous as fuck.)* No! NO, I didn't have you! False gods had you! Success, security, safety, settling had you. They had turned you into a littl' bitch. And I wasn't having that.

NO!

Not with my Beloved!

(Cold as ice.) So I killed them. I removed EVERYTHING that was not of me from you. And I would do it again, KNOWING you would come to my house and spit fire in my face.

(She starts weeping. God softens. He gets out of his chair, and a host of angels stand up when he stands. He walks over to her and kneels in front of her. He wipes her tears away and speaks in the gentlest voice he has.)

You were dying, Beloved. You were buried under a life that took more than it gave you. That's not my will. That's not my will for your life. I created the heavens and earth for you, Venus. You are my wild child. I know you are jealous of Jesus. I understand. Jesus is my grace and mercy. You, my Precious One, you are my wrath. You are that aspect of me that burns this bitch to the ground on GP alone.

You were losing that. You were getting soft. Becoming digestible.

(Standing straight up and walking to the window to look out at the sun, earth, moons, and stars all burning bright at the same time.) I will be damned if my Chosen One will dim her light, abdicate her power, or walk in any sort of fear. No. Not mine. So when you prayed that prayer, I knew it was time to bring you back to me.

Me: *(She hears her God and understands.)* But I don't know who I am anymore.

God: *(Quietly. Breathing life into the empty shell of his Beloved.)* Yes, you do.
You are the aspect of me that most human beings are incapable of fucking with.
You are an Old Testament chick living in a New Testament world.
You are the Alpha and Omega.
The I Am that I am.
You are the beginning and the end.
You are the beginning that was the Word.
You are the law.
You are my justice.
My wrath.
My vengeance.
You are my purity.
You are my Truth.
You are my uncompromising love and my ruthless atonement.
You are the fire I rained down on Sodom and Gomorrah for disrespecting me.
You are my hand of Death that took David's illegitimate child despite his cries.
You are the horns that brought the Walls of Jericho down.

You are the seven plagues that had Pharaoh let my people go.
You are the wind that parted the Red Sea.
You are my tears turned to rain that made Noah's ark float.
You are the patience I placed in Job.

THAT'S who the fuck you are. You. Are. Me.

Me: *(She sits quietly. Still. Being with it all. She looks God in the eye.)* Ok, Lord. I hear you. And I understand, but... what am I supposed to do with my life now?

God: *(Waves to Gabriel to pour him another drink. Gabriel does his will. God sips it slowly and whispers.)* Nothing.

Me: *(Shocked)* NOTHING.

God: I birthed you in violence. I spat you out in a world constituted in pain. I orchestrated every bad thing that has happened to you in your existence. Everything that you have gone through was my doing; my will for your life. And no matter the shame, degradation, betrayal, heartbreak, or deceit, *your heart remains pure.* Just like Jesus. I know you are jealous of your brother, but he had his purpose, and so do you.

So you don't have to do anything. Allow it. Allow it to arise.
Me: But what about my company, my calling—

God: Let it go.

Me: WHAT?????? *(Dizzy with disbelief.)*

God: Let it all go. None of that matters. It was just your training ground. All of it. I have created you in my image, not to redeem the world but to make it anew. You were created to annihilate the lies that people have come to believe as truths.

The first time I destroyed the world, I used rain. When I told you I would come again, what did I say?

Me: *(Remembering as if waking up from a coma.)* You said you would rain down fire.

God: Yes. Fire is truth. You are the Truth. My truth. I created you for this. So now my Beloved, in whom I am well pleased, you tell me. Tell me who the fuck you are?

Me: *(She gets it now. She looks God directly in the eye and sees how much he loves her. That he chose her over billions and billions of other souls to groom for this extraordinary purpose. She remembers all the times he was walking with her in the fiery furnace called the streets and how he never left her.)*

I am my father's daughter.

(God sees his daughter, his most treasured creation come home to him and his heart breaks. He opens his arms; they turn into wings big enough to lift her to his chest. The angels start singing, and Gabriel looks over at Jesus and winks. Jesus and the Holy Spirit smile. Their sister has come home.)

3/16/19

Real & Raw Series
Hate

DISCLAIMER: I am sad, not suicidal. Please do not post ANY reference to me seeing or getting a therapist (done), that I need to pray or trust God (covered on both fronts) or that I am depressed. I am grieving the way writing artists grieve: I write. I write for me, not for you.

I write what is true for me.

It helps me feel better and process all I have lost: my womb, my marriage, my sense of self. This is a poem. It is not a covert cry for help. So please ONLY post if you are empathizing, celebrating, or offering insight that empowers me as a human being. I deeply welcome quality, thoughtful responses, or reflections. They help me.

Sharing my inner world is a sacred trust. I allow you into the pages of my emotional diary—it is privileged to access. Respect it. Please.

I say this with love: If you cannot honor my boundaries and you post some bullshit, I will delete it and block you from my page. I promise. #breathefire

~~~~~~

One breath. Two pulls.

It's quiet on the inside.
Silence comes after wailing.

I have never had what I wanted.
I have had what I should have.
What others wanted for me.

What someone I loved wanted—so I wanted it.

I don't deserve to have what I want.

I have failed so much, so often, I am afraid to dream.

Afraid to stand for me.
For my dreams.
My wants.
My heart's desire.

Who would give them to me?

Stand for me?
March for me?
Live for me?
Die for me?

I have never stood for me, so why should someone else?

When I was on the streets, it would hurt me to see someone I loved in pain. So I took the hit or went without to protect someone I called my own. Where I come from, you show your love through actions.

Don't snitch.
Take the fall.
Have your back.
If I have, you have.
I got five on it.
Puff, puff, pass.
Share gear.
Hold my piece.
If I die, take care of my momma.

So I got in the habit of putting my body in harm's way to protect people. To show them—momma, brother, sister, cousin, friend, soldier, roommate, teammate, peer, lover, spouse, team, client—the truth of my love.

I have loved what and whom I call my own with a fierce love.
My love was fierce but blind.
I never saw that the love was not reciprocated.
It was only tolerated.

The love I gave for free became an expectation.
Then obligation.
Then entitlement.

I think I thought that if I showed you that I loved you,
then you would love me with the same kind of blind loyalty I loved you.

I was wrong.
You don't love me.
You don't.

I don't mean you don't think you love me. But you only love me when it's convenient. Your love is that Peter kind of love: passionately professed in private but denied three times by midnight in public. I am a loveless shell of skin, bone, and ragged breath. I know I am supposed to love me, but how, Lord?

How do you love something that is dead on the inside?
Something that is so not there,
anyone can fill it, and it takes the shape
of the new person's needs in order to be needed?

I am an emotional chameleon, shapeshifting to become whatever and whoever I need to be in order for you to love me.

Maybe if I hold my breath until the veins in my neck bulge and my eyes explode into dozens of tiny, frozen, diamond-shaped crystals, carving tracks of tears down my cheeks to my chin, you would take my hands and pull me into a silence beneath grief.

Beyond self-doubt.
Behind hopelessness.
Hopelessness is the barren soil
that births self-hate.

Self-hate isn't loud.
It's quiet. Steady. Insidious.
It shows up in the thousand paper cuts of compromise.
Acquiescing.
Making it work.
Self-sacrifice.
Until the you that loved so fiercely
no longer exists.

Self-hate annihilates the self.
Hate is not the opposite of love.
Hate is the absence of love.
It is distance, despondent, cold.

Hate is devoid of life.

Hate kills life by eating away the color in my cheeks…

...the light in my eyes...
...the smile in my voice...
...one breath at a time.

by Venus Opal Reese (vor)

3/20/19

(Truth) I was not going to post this piece. I was going to submit it to publication outlets that require previously unpublished work. When I was informed that posting counts as "published," I was pissed.

So if I wanted my word to reach more people, I would have to "submit."

I felt like I was about to subject myself to the tyranny of being picked. That felt like begging for inclusion and validation. But I do want more people to read my Word. So I wrote two new pieces and read them online but didn't post the words to receive your response, wisdom, and thoughtful reflections. And I missed you. I missed you terribly.

I am writing myself into wellness.

And to NOT include you in each step of my healing felt like a lie. No. I'm not selling out to fit into other people's boxes. Even the writer box called submission guidelines.

My copywriter helped me. She recommended I keep writing myself into existence and when I feel compelled to write something for publication to do so or take a piece and change it by 20 percent, so it's like a new piece. She and her team are going to organize my writings and put them on Medium, so my Word leaves me.

I don't want to market.
I don't want to sell.
Right now, I just want to share.
Sharing is how I'm healing.

And I love sharing… with you…

I need you.

Your eyes.
Your insight.
You.

Thank you for holding space and walking with me while I resurrect myself. I love you.

Real & Raw Series
Addiction

Not all addicts look like junkies.

When I started to make money as an entrepreneur, I was hanging out with rich White Men CEOs. These men brought in over $50 million in annual sales. And they were good men. Kind. Honest. Upright. They listened to my Word as truth and enveloped me into their fold.

And it was warm.

Dinner. Parties. Happy hour. Drinks. Lots of drinks.

They were buying, so I said yes. #ghettoiknow

One of the CEOs introduced me to wines. He taught me all about wines—color, legs, tannin, body, vineyards, notes—everything. I was flattered, but more than anything, I was insecure. Actually, I felt inferior. He had so much more than I had ever been able to imagine—until I was included in his world.

So I took to drinking wine because it made me feel rich.

I thought it made me look sophisticated when I ordered a Riesling or a Pinot Noir, swirling the pretty colored liquid around in an elegant, oversized wine glass, sniffing it, and sipping samples for the table.

In my mind, wine wasn't alcohol.

Alcohol was Mad Dog 20/20 in a brown paper bag.
Or Hennessey and Coke in a mason jar.
Or Colt 45 in a ceramic mug.

Wine was some shit we drank at church once a month for communion.

So, I didn't relate to wine as booze.

I come from a family of addicts. It's in my DNA. I had lost my oldest sister to heroin laced with embalming fluid. So I didn't do drugs. But I knew their damage firsthand. I remember a neighbor, Ms. Thang, on the block who drank so much so regularly, the stench of week-old vodka seeped through her pores. Slap Happy was called that because he slapped himself in the face every few seconds to keep from nodding off.

Wine wasn't hard liquor. It wasn't dope.

I wasn't like Ms. Thang or Slap Happy...

...until one day, I was sitting in my Lexus drinking a bottle of wine from a brown paper bag.

I am an alcoholic.
An addict.

I drank to feel like I was confident.
I drank to feel like I was just as important as the rich White Men who had befriended me.
I drank to numb the rawness of my insecurity.
I drank to hide my inferiority.
I drank to cover up that I was a fraud, that I was a street urchin, and didn't have a right to be in this crowd.

My CEOs fed me business. And the more money I made, the more I felt insecure, inferior, and like a fraud.

The more I drank.

Until one day sitting in the dark in my Lexus, holding a half-empty bottle of wine, hands shaking, to my quivering lips, crying, I realized I couldn't stop.

I am an addict.

My addiction started way before I became a millionaire. Way before CEOs. Way before becoming an entrepreneur.

My addiction is rooted in my wants. Wants that have their roots in my childhood.

Wants are created in a moment of crisis to self-soothe. At least my wants were.

When I was sleeping in alleys, infested with maggots, roaches, and rats, I fantasized about living in a mansion with a White maid (a nice one like the one on *Diff'rent Strokes*) in a soft bed with designer pillows and matching sheets.

When I would get clothes from a church, Goodwill, or the garbage (that I would hand wash in the bathroom sink at the Greyhound bus station in downtown Baltimore), I dreamt about having brand new clothes from the fancy stores in the movies like *Pretty Woman*—with the tags still on them.

To this day, I leave the tags on clothes I buy to prove I bought them AND the tag ensures that it is new.

I grew up in squalor and knew survival intimately—up close. Personal. So in my young mind, the only way out was to be "Big." I wanted to be "Big," and that meant being on TV. Pretty clothes. Pretty home. Food every day. People being nice to me. Praise. Affection.

Big = Rich —> Famous

Famous meant being on TV.

And I have chased that dream EVER since.

Like an addict.

I sacrificed EVERYTHING to be "somebody."

I got MASTERFUL at seeing through lies, sniffing out survival strategies, and knee-jerk reactions.
I became MASTERFUL at hearing EVERYTHING people are NOT saying. I can listen so deeply, I "hear" others' wounds, resentments, secret desires, betrayals, violations, and dreams. I can sit with ANYONE and, within seconds, if not minutes, know EXACTLY what you want.

I could "read" a john and know if he would hit a woman or if he was grieving the loss of his recently deceased wife. The term "comfort woman" is real. I got MASTERFUL at helping people see what could be, what THEY wanted instead of the pissy mattress and condemned row house they called home.

I got so good at this, people started to notice.
I became useful.
Especially when it came to money.

I could see what to say to ANYONE to have him or her want something they didn't want the moment before. It could be a drink, a dime bag, or some bootleg clothes sold from the trunk of a car or out of a backroom or basement.

Decades later, Nanna told me I was built for two things: words and making money. She was 100 percent right.

I wanted to be "Big." Big in my little Black girl logic was being on TV. But in order to be on TV, I would need to bland me out to be digestible for a mass audience. And I tried.

I have four degrees, including a second master's degree and a Ph.D. from Stanford University.

I taught in the university and became a tenured professor. I have trained tens of thousands of leaders as a professor, program leader, artist, writer, and social media influencer.

I became an entrepreneur and grossed over $5,000,000 with no "formal" business training, without loans, government funding, investors, or a sales team.

I got married in Maui, bought a mansion, a Mercedes, and a Lexus.

I BECAME the American fuckin' dream.

But no matter WHAT I did, I never made it.

As an addict, one has cravings. I was feignin' for being "Big." So I "dummied down the street in me to fit in. To make it. To be "somebody."

I kept trying to make myself "mainstream," but I am not built for that.

I am street-trained. Born and bred.

We don't fit into structures never built for us. We break shit down to its rawest essence. We don't obey the law. We break it. We make new laws. And we die for them. Physically. Mentally. Emotionally. Spiritually. Familiarly. Communally. Financially.

I don't have to look like a junkie to be an addict.

Seeking approval is an addiction.
Needing to be needed is an addiction.
Success at any cost is an addiction.
Over-giving is an addiction.
Self-sacrifice is an addiction.
Working hard is an addiction.
Being less-than is an addiction.
Walking through the world as not-enough is an addiction.
Having to do it my way is an addiction.
Being right and/or righteous is an addiction.

All of these addictions in service of my want to be Big. Mainstream. Rich. Famous. "Somebody." Important. Wanted. Loved—

I wanted to be loved.

Big = Loved.

Being loved was all I ever wanted. I wanted to be wanted. I wanted to know what it felt like to be loved. Momma didn't want me. She would have aborted me if my father hadn't first stopped her, then the penal system. Later, she would have killed me herself if I hadn't acquiesced over and over again.

My addiction to wanting to be "Big" almost killed me. It had me burn out my body, burn through relationships, and sell out my soul.
Wants are created in a moment of crisis to self-soothe.
What I want and what I am built for are two different things.
I am built for two things: words (written/spoken) and making money.

What if I stop feeding my addiction to wanting to be wanted and started to pour ALL of my attention to just writing, to speaking my truth?

What if I gave up my wanting to be big and just wrote and spoke for a living?

What if I...
...never became Big
...was never on TV or famous
...never made another million again
...just did what I was built for.

What would it be like to turn my addiction inward?

To crave my own approval? My own peace? To jones for my own self-expression and fulfillment instead of trying to get it through other people's flesh or social status approval? To be a junkie for my joy? To feign for me—instead of trying to have someone outside of me do so?

Maybe I can swap addictions: trade "Big" for "built for?"

Would it work?

I don't know.

But I am willing to try...

Venus Opal Reese (vor)

3/25/19

Real & Raw Series
Stand

Each time I stand for myself, I feel afraid.

My birth mother was a wounded and malicious woman. She had been raised in violence and had perfected the art of justified cruelty.

Momma was most malicious, not when I was on the floor in the fetal position, shielding my frail frame from "you brought it on your damn self" kicks.

Momma was her most malicious when I wouldn't cry.

She could beat me until I was dizzy from pain, but I'd be damned if I cried...

...until the pain became so searing, my body bypassed my will, and I crumpled into an abyss of tears just to make her stop.

So as I learn to stand for myself, I feel this hovering, fluttering "uh oh" feeling each time I say "no" to other people's agendas and "yes" to me.

My body can't tell the difference between a real, remembered, or imagined threat.

It stills braces itself due to the surprise attack from dozens of cops stampeding our home on Henneman Ave. in Baltimore. They were looking for a big-time drug dealer who was a "friend" of the family. They didn't catch him, but when they drew their guns and aimed them at me, screaming. "Don't move! Put your hands up!" I froze. My body wouldn't move—then it began to shake uncontrollably. I held my breath to not move, to not make them shoot me. It worked.

I had learned not to draw attention to myself... or I ran the risk of running right into a fist...
...or a backhanded slap.
...or an extension cord whip.
...or a broomstick beating.
...or periodic starvation for not cleaning the tub right.
...or being locked in a room for days.

I learned not to stand for myself out loud.

So I did so underground. On the hush. The down low.

I became subversive.

Defiant in silence.
I was willing to take the hit for what I deemed fair.
Right.
Just.
True.

Standing up for myself cost me... It had me...

Pushed downstairs.
Pushed through walls.
Pushed out of a moving car.

It was dangerous standing for myself.

So I acquiesced. I played nice—to survive.

Years, decades later, I'm still surviving. When I stand for myself out loud, when I say "no" to people, places, and plans that no longer serve me, I STILL feel exposed—like I am about to be hit for doing something I didn't even know was bad.

Every time I stand for myself, my body begins to shake and curl inward to prepare for being hurt.

I have as much right to stand for myself, to say "no," to change my mind, to look out for me as much as anybody else.

I matter too.

I matter to me.

I matter enough to myself to go through the physiological, mental, and emotional anguish designed to keep me quiet, and in my place, so they knew themselves as power.

I am tired of feeling afraid.

No. That's not true. I am tired of trying not to feel afraid.

In my body, there are memories, scars, burns, that I can't emotionally erase. I feel them wake up each time I do something for me. Each time I put my feelings, my wants, my needs before another.

They are there, they are a part of me. They are as much a part of me as the texture of my hair, the color of my skin, and my height.

So I embrace them.
Whenever my physiology takes over and I brace my body for the inevitable blow, I let my body feel afraid and remind myself that I am safe now.

It's safe to stand for myself.
It's safe to be happy.
It's safe to be pretty.
It's safe to have my woman's body.
It's safe to laugh out loud.
It's safe to feel joy.

I am learning to stand for me with me. It sounds a bit like this.

"It's safe to be happy, Venus. It's safe to have what you want. It's safe to be alive. To feel good. To laugh. You're not in danger anymore. You don't have to make nice to keep the peace or suffer in silence, hoping for favor. You are your father's daughter. You are God wrapped in flesh. You are brave. They can't hurt you now. Never again."

I just realized that perhaps standing is standing for myself within.

I attracted violence. Pain. Punishment from others because I don't have standards for myself to stand for—so I fell for anything that looked like love.

Standing up is actually standing for me with me. So I never have people in my life who can act out their violence on me—in any form—ever again.

Standing for myself is setting an internal standard that puts me at the center of my life, my joy, my peace. Everything and everyone else gets to stay at the margins.

Setting a standard for myself with myself about myself so I am impervious to others' emotional manipulations, cowardly sucker punches, or passive-aggressive takeaways is how I stand for me.

Yes, I stand for me... Knowing the takers will sling rocks and arrows at me.

I stand for me... clear that it will cost me something—just like it did with Momma— but it will earn me my self-respect.

I stand for me... knowing I may lose everything I have given my life to—and that's ok.

I stand for me because I matter to me.
I stand for me because I am the first example of teaching others how to treat me.
I stand for me because I need to know I am on my side even if I do it wrong.
I stand for me as an act of defiance.
I stand for me, afraid and courageous, and brave. I stand for me because I can.

I stand for me simply because I say so.

I am not a little girl anymore. I am a woman who knows things and has a track record of getting up off the mat.

If I count all the times I have been knocked to my knees—I also have to embrace how each time I got back up.

Perhaps I have ALWAYS stood for me. But I didn't count it. Maybe my very nature is to stand. I don't know.

What I do know is I refuse to live in fear.

I am unwilling to live my life being afraid.

From this breath forward, I choose to live brave.

Venus Opal Reese (vor)

3/30/19

(Truth) A male friend, let's call him Mr. Man, took me to lunch last week, and we got into an argument. Actually, I started to fuss at Mr. Man for not doing what he said he would and not telling me. His reason pissed me off. It was pride. Pure, unadulterated masculine pride. I told him the truth: when you don't do what you say, by when you say you will, it erodes the trust I have in you.

And I told him he was dominating me.

Mr. Man takes care of me emotionally, literally, and in my business. I told him how much I need him. Especially in this season. What I asked him to do was in service of him. It hurt me that he can take care of me, but he wouldn't let me love him the way I love: by supporting him to have what HE wants. He heard me and made a new promise. And kept it.

I told him I loved him. He said he knew. I said, "no, you don't." He said, "then write it down; write down why you love me." So I did. The piece below was written for Mr. Man, but it actually shows us as women what it looks like to be loved by a (Black) Man who loves you for no reason. Women in general, but Black Women more specifically, don't know what it looks like when a healed, whole, and transformed Black Man loves you purely—no agenda, no angle, and no transaction.

Mr. Man has transformed how I see and relate to Black Men. My father saved my life and left. Mr. Man empowers my life by staying. The consistency of his love heals a missing I didn't know I had.

Challenge: I invite every woman who reads this piece to share it with a man who has demonstrated time and time again that he loves you. I think he will appreciate you for doing so. :-)

Thank you, Mr. Man. I love you.
#foreverandforalways #norequestnodemand

Real & Raw Series
Covered

You are a man.

A good man.

A Black Man who treats me like I am precious.

You take care of me.
You listen, and you get up under my dreams.
You support me in such a way, I feel safe and cherished.
You spoil me, and you don't take your love away when I do.
You forgive me without ever asking me to apologize.
You carry my weight to lighten the load of the calling on my life.

I can tell you the truth, and you never judge me.

I don't know what I ever did to deserve your loyalty or devotion, but I thank God you choose me to love so relentlessly.

I love you for being my safe haven in the storms of life.
I love you for taking care of me when I cannot.
I love you for demonstrating through your actions your belief in me.

You are my friend, my confidant, my caretaker, my protector, my provider, my comic relief, my net when I fall, my strong tower when I need to lean in, my eyes when I can't see straight, my voice when my throat is swollen shut with hurt, anger, or fear.

You soften me.

Because I trust you, I let my guard down.

I tell you the truth because I can trust you with my secrets... and my dreams.

Simply put, I love you because you love me...

You love me like I am worth it.
You love me like I am worth loving.
You love me like I deserve to be loved just because I breathe.

I have never had a man in my life love me as you do.
Fully.
Unconditionally.
Consistently.

You love me back to wholeness.
You cast vision over my life, and you hold the space until I step into what you see for me.

I am so very grateful you love all of me—my wounds, my genius, my fire.
You are fast becoming my created standard for the men in my life instead of what I was born into.

You redefine Black Man/Masculinity for me.

You have become my normal for letting myself be
- loved
- cherished
- celebrated
- supported
- spoiled
- seen

- heard
- empowered
- taken care of
- nurtured
- guided
- influenced

by the men who love me.

Thank you for being whatever I need at the moment I need it.

You help me not quit on me.
You learn new things to grow with me.
You always treat me like a lady.
A princess.
A queen.
A goddess.

You give me your undivided attention—and it means the world to me…

You hold my hand when I am afraid and take me out, so I don't feel so lonely.

You feed me, and you listen to me—at the same time.

You won't take a dime from me—no matter how many times I offer. You ALWAYS pay—for food, gas, flights, investing in MY programs, hotels. My money is no good with you. And I am grateful.

You keep your promises to me, and you hear me out when my feelings are hurt—and I love you for doing so.

I love you.

More than a brother.
Beyond a lover.
In a space that lives in the unsaid.

You cover me.

I don't know why you love me...
...but I thank God that you do...

Venus Opal Reese (vor)

3/31/19

Real & Raw Series

Artist

I wrote a new piece called "Stand" and heard the phrase, "but some of us are brave" when I finished. The phrase is part of the title of a book that was originally published in 1982, called *All the Women Are White, All the Blacks Are Men, But Some of Us Are Brave: Black Women's Studies.* It is the first comprehensive collection of Black feminist scholarship. I read it in grad school, and its impact was profound. It helped shape me as an artist and a scholar.

I found the book on Amazon. I looked at the cover of the book, then read the back of it. Just rereading the back cover and meandering through the table of contents pushed me back into memory. My educational walk. Before Stanford, I graduated from Ohio State University with my MFA. Before OSU, I graduated from Adelphi University with my BFA. This (re)memory brought to my consciousness how the women who wrote books, danced, or created art did it for me.

Black Women Feminist poets, artists, choreographers, novelists, and scholars are the ones who birthed me as a performative scholar. Audre Lorde, bell hooks, Barbara Smith, Barbara Christian, Alice Walker, Angela Davis, Ntozake Shange, Urban Bush Women, Sweet Honey In The Rock, Anna Deavere Smith, Virginia Hamilton, and Mildred D. Taylor. These women's work shaped me. They wrote for me, even though they never met me. They told my story. They gave me a space to write myself into existence in my own image.

I didn't go to school for education, aspiration, or to better myself. I went to school because I could eat. Educational institutions gave me a safe and warm place to sleep, and all I had to do was make good grades. It felt like a good deal, coming up off the streets. So I went. From Northwestern High School in Baltimore, Maryland, to Stanford University in Palo Alto, California, my education was never aspirational; it was always functional.

I went to primarily "White" schools. Nanna made sure of that. She said because I came up on the streets, and had primarily lived in "Black" ghettos, I needed to learn how to "deal" with White people. #hollaifyoufeelme

White people/White privilege/Whiteness/ was invisible to me until I went to college. I knew I was poor, but I didn't know I was Black until I went to college. There was so much "White" everywhere—the food, the language, the clothes, the cliques, the standards, the expectations, the privilege, the favor, the grace given by default—that my "Blackness" had to get loud to survive the erasure of my very presence.

I felt so disappeared I went internal. I was so lonely I went to the one comfort I had when I was living in Momma's house, then on the streets: libraries. I went to the library on campus to find books about Black Women, films, poetry readings, dance concerts on campus to help me stay the course. Books have saved my life more than once.

It's because of the energetic space these Black Women Feminists provided me; cradling me in the pages and creases of books, caressing me with the silky texture of their songs, and seducing me with the eloquence of their bodies moving through the air like poetry, that I survived my education.

Ntozake's "For Colored Girls Who Have Considered Suicide When the Rainbow Is Enuf" was the model for my first solo performance piece at Adelphi, where I did my undergraduate degree in theatre. I wasn't being cast in lead roles because I wasn't White.

My teachers helped.

One teacher gave me Ntozake's choreopoem, and another teacher encouraged me to write my own work and perform it at our college pub. I did both, and I was set free. No longer did I have to go through the internal anxiety of auditioning, praying to be picked, but knowing deep in my heart that I wouldn't be. I could write. I wrote my way out of the typecast of "maid," "mammy," and "Foxy Brown."

And I performed.

I discovered I had comic timing and could make people feel things with my words. Plus, it gave me the freedom to say my truth to an audience who wanted to hear me. As the only Black student in an entirely White department, I had created a much-needed space to speak my truth and be witnessed. By mostly White audiences.

I became "Black" in Ohio.

My undergrad was at Adelphi University, which was a rich White school. Rich White folk don't have to flex. They know they have everything, so there's no need to make their whiteness felt. At OSU, I encountered the working class and poor Whites. Whiteness was a badge of honor they spit-shined on a daily basis by humiliating me, isolating me, and undermining me in subtle but clear ways. Their White was painful. So painful, I retreated into silence and books just to stay out of harm's way.

My silence did not protect me.

I was getting my first master's in acting and movement theatre with an emphasis on choreography and mime. Guest artists, professors, and industry stars celebrated the work I created. A famous playwright took to me and made me the lead actress of a world premiere. I was in the paper and doing well in my classes. I wasn't doing it the way others were, and that felt wrong to my peers. I was getting too big for my britches. That's when the ugly came out of the closet. I ran right smack dab into the brick wall of overt racism. It killed my spirit. I took my isolation, their righteous contempt (personified in fake smiles dripping with poisonous drool), and cruel diminishment out on my body.

I starved myself. Down to 99 lbs.

It was bell hooks, *Sisters of the Yam: Black Women and Self-Recovery* that gave me the language, the tools, and the will to live again.

Writing became my weapon of resistance to systemic racism.

When I write my truth, I realize I am in a long literary tradition of Black Women who stood for me as an artist, as a scholar (which is an art form just as rigorous as ballet) before I was even born. They knew I would come, so they made a place for me at the table. Actually, they made me a new table that makes room for me to be my whole self.

Because they stood for me, I now can stand.
I stand by writing my truth. When I write my truth, I honor their stand for me, my artistry, my voice, my life. Their stand for me was/is political. My writing makes it personal. By writing my truth, I am revolting—just like the lineage of Black Women of which I am an offspring did— uprising against each and every way I have been put in my place.

I am the insurrection.
The resurrection.
The second fuckin' coming.

Give me a minute.
Let me get my breath back.

Then watch me...

...watch me stand.

Venus Opal Reese (vor)

4/2/19

Real & Raw Series
Pimp

(I apologize.) I took this down because I was scared you would judge me. I apologize for not trusting you. You said you love me, and I have permission to be my whole self. I got scared and ran.

I'm back now.

I read a few of the encouraging comments and called my best friend. I got my courage up. And I remembered you have been with me the whole way. Why would you turn your back on me now? Thank you for your loyalty and for not judging me. I didn't realize how much bravery it takes to heal... thank you for walking with me... all. The. Way.

WARNING: THIS WRITING CONTAINS PROFANITY, EXPLICIT SEXUAL LANGUAGE, AND SEXUAL CONTENT. If you have ANY wounds around sexual trauma, be it personal, witnessed, participation in, or it happened to a loved one, I strongly advise: DO NOT READ THIS POST. It will trigger you. It will upset you, and it will evoke a visceral reaction.

So, as an act of self-love, please don't gamble with your well-being. Don't read this.

Read my other work. Don't fuck with this one. It was hard for me to write, so I KNOW it's going to be hard for those of us who have been violated, under the auspices of love, for you to read. So please, don't be strong, and don't doubt my recommendation. I know what I wrote. And it's designed to rip away the husks that hide. I love you enough to do my best to protect you AND write my truth.

So please—for the love of God and all things holy, love yourself enough to not go there. You will not survive this one.

It was written to annihilate.

COMMENTS: This is a piece of erotica. Please make sure your comments are substantive, not juvenile. I look forward to your insights, reflections, and wisdom.

~~~~~~~~~~~~~~~~~~~~~~~~~~~~~~~~~~~~~~~

There was a man she thought loved her.

She didn't realize it at the time, but he was a pimp.

An emotional pimp.

People get it twisted. Pimpin' isn't about sex.

It's about control.
Emotional control.
If you can control a woman's feelings, her body will follow.

So will her loyalty.

A good pimp doesn't have to hit or force his women to do his bidding.

If he has mastered the art, we do it because we love him.

An emotional pimp is a collector. He can only tolerate broken things.

Women, boys, little girls who have turned their backs on themselves because life had already turned their backs on them.

So he collects women who were broken, fatherless, without a home.

Or he finds a weakness to exploit for his own personal gain.

He traffics in power. He peddles pleasure.

He knows how to seduce; to have women fall in love so he can turn their love into currency.

A good pimp is brilliant. He understands EXACTLY what you need to hear to have you take an action that makes you more and more his possession. He is amoral and empathetic. We have to believe he loves us in order to take his word over everyone else's.

For the weak among us, after being "loved" by him, we try to commit suicide.

He pimps pleasure.
He punishes with his absence.

No call.
No reason.
No touch.

Just silence. Withdrawal. Absence.

Love cannot sustain itself without his presence.

So her own heart compelled her to get back in his good graces.

She calls.
She knocks.
She stands outside his door for hours. Days.

He makes her wait.
He wants her to beg.
To drive herself crazy with worry and doubt that he has left her for good.

Hours. Days. Weeks go by.

Then one day, he shows up. Looking like money. Smelling like dollars.

He dresses his ass off—from the money his women give him. A Caesar low cut fade. Edged up. Sporting new brown leather shoes, matching belt, brown and blue sports jacket, crisp white shirt, and a blue silk tie to contrast the brown. His look is replete with a precisely folded pocket square and customized cufflinks. He's beautiful. Big eyes that see too much, full lips practiced at pulling out of women secrets they didn't know they had.

"Open the door. I heard you've been looking for me." Liar. He knows she has been reaching out to him for weeks. He knows because he has watched her. He always watches from afar. Lurking in the shadows. Making friends with her friends to keep tabs. Slow roll in his black Escalade, late-night drive-bys in the rain, when she is walking. He watches to see when she is about to let go and move on—that's when he shows up.

Good pimpin' is a game of mental chess. It's a strategy. The game is to get her to want him so badly, she forgets how he fucked over her and left her out there—cold and alone.

So he starts. First, it's just a lean on the doorframe. Next, it's a casual touch on the arm. He lets her say her piece, as he gets closer and closer to her skin. She's angry and relieved at the same time. He strokes her hair and starts to whisper to her. That she is so beautiful. And smart. And sexy. That she deserves to be treated like a queen.

He squeezes her hands. Her arm. Her thigh...

She feels her body swelling. He can smell her scent.

He makes a safe space for her to tell him the truth. How much she loves him and how she has missed him. Painfully so. As she confesses, he touches her softly, tenderly whispering how he has missed her... how she is his best friend... how much he needs her...

"What do I have to do, Daddy, to make you love me again?"

"You've been a bad girl..."

"I'm sorry, Daddy. Please. Tell me what to do. I need you. I love you. I am so sorry."

"Take off your clothes."

"Daddy, please, I didn't mean to—"

"Take them off."

"Yes, daddy."

"Get on your knees, bitch." It sounds like a caress...

"Yes, Daddy."

"You know better than to disobey me."

"I'm sorry—I thought you wanted—"

"Shhhhh. You make me punish you. I love you, baby. Why do you make me do this? It hurts me to hurt you." Pimps ALWAYS make it your fault. It's NEVER them.

He slowly takes off his belt.

"Put your hands behind your back, baby... please."

"Yes, Daddy."

"Lift your legs up."

"Yes, Daddy... I am sorr—"

"Shhhhh... hush. Let me take care of you. Let me please you... You want this... this is why you disrespect me... you want me to fuck you like a bitch. Treat you like a slut. You want this. Say you want this. Tell your daddy you want this."

"I want this, Daddy... I want you..."

He hog-ties her hands and feet behind her back.

Then he lays in front of her face with his breath caressing her cheek as he talks to her.

"You belong to me. You are mine. I love you. When you talk back to me or don't obey, you disrespect the only person in the world who loves you. Who could ever love you? I saved you. Haven't I been there for you?" His voice is soft, and he starts to touch her, fondle her. The tenderness of his touch brings tears to her eyes.

"I am so sorry. I didn't mean to disrespect you. I didn't mean to make you angry."

"Shhhhh... I know. But you did, and you have to pay."

He takes off his beautiful tie and wraps it around her neck, gently.

"You belong to me. Nobody else wants you. Your momma didn't want you. She turned you out. I was the one who saved you. And you act like you think you are better than me, smarter than me. But you are not." He gets behind her, threads the tie through the belt, and gently pulls it as he fingers her wet pussy. She gasps. Tears run down her cheeks. He inhales her. She can hear his breathing change. Her body ripens…

"See, your body wants me. You want me. Tell me you love me."

He enters her from the back, all the while gently pulling his tie.

"I want you to have my baby. That's how much I love you. I am going to cum inside of you. So all day, you will feel me seeping out of your pussy, and you will think of me. You will imagine carrying my child. Having my baby. Do you want that? Do you want to have my baby?"

"Yes… yes… I… dooooo. o.o.o.o Daaaaaadddddddddddyyyyyyy…"

A good pimp, one who has mastered the art, ALWAYS has his women feel special, like she is the only one—even though she knows she is not. But in her heart, she believes—knows—he loves her special. And it's that knowing that makes her his slave.
They climax together.

He unties her and pulls her close to him.

He bathes her in scented water and tends to her body with Egyptian musk oil. He makes her feel beautiful. Sensual. His.

She BELONGS to him.

And she will do whatever he wants her to do.
No force.

It feels like it's her idea.

And besides, who else would want her? She's not pretty or smart.
Who else would understand her appetites?
Her fears?
Her insecurities?

She needs him.

He made sure of it.

~~~~~~

He has a habit of leaving.

But each time he leaves her, she gets stronger.

She starts to see the pattern.

And she learns.
She learns how to pimp.

She learns how to walk away and stay away until he wants her.

Needs her.

Begs her.

She lies in wait for the perfect moment to strike.

To hurt him like he has hurt her.

She becomes MASTERFUL at pleasure. Men. Women. Both.
She can change the pace of her breathing and make a man cum.

She becomes a bad bitch. And she knows it.

So does he.

"Open the door."

"No."

"What are you afraid of, Daddy? I won't hurt you."

"Leave me alone."

"Open the fucking door. NOW!" He obeys. He is broken too.

"Take off your clothes."

"No."

She looks at him and tilts her head. She sees the damaged little boy in him. She sees the little boy who was molested by a woman when he was nine. The little boy who was held down while his little boy face was forced between her greedy grown-ass woman thighs. He survived the woman by closing his eyes.

But it tarnished him.

Turned him cruel on the inside. From nine to now, he hates women. He became a bully. She sees a wounded nine-year-old boy in a grown man's body, making every woman he meets his bitch. She sees the weakness in his jaw. She sees that he is a coward who uses sex to feel like he has control.

She starts to whisper to him. Telling him secrets that make him feel special. She touches him softly. Gentle. She pats his face. She strokes his hair. He relaxes. He can only relax when he feels complete submission. When he is related to like a god.

She takes off her clothes, except her heels, and walks to his dressing closet. She rummages around until she finds what she was looking for.

"Sit with me, Daddy. Let me take care of you. Let me please you. I love you. Do you love me?"

"Yes, baby."

"Then let me take care of you. Just close your eyes and relax. Let me love you."

He closes his eyes, and she blindfolds him with a blue silk tie.

She pulls his pants down to his knees, pushes him back on the king-size bed, and straddles him.

"No touch." She rubs her breast on his shirt and face. He moans. She lets her wetness seep through his shirt on his belly.

He reaches for her.

"No touch."

He relaxes.

She takes him inside of her—her mouth, her wetness—until he is panting, squirming, sweating...

But she won't let him cum.

She tantalizes him for hours.

Until he is a ball of raw nerves shaking, quivering on the bed...

She takes his blindfold off. She sees the yearning in his eyes... and something else. She sees the little boy in him. Something in her softens.

"I love you."

I know. I love you too."

Then she does something neither one of them ever thought was possible.

She gets dressed and leaves.

He is shocked. Numb. Dumbfounded—his pants down around his ankles. The blue silk tie, on the floor, crumpled. Just like his heart. And he weeps. The love of his life just walked out the door. He can hear her heels, confidently walking down the hallway. He can smell her musk on his breath and face. He can taste her, his her, on his lips.
He knows she loves herself now more than she loves him. And that she will never come back.

She loved him enough to let him go...

...and set herself free.

Venus Opal Reese (vor)

(Requesting Wisdom) This is a long one. Just trying to see if I am wanting too much for myself. For all of my successful entrepreneurs who are also Creatives, please share.
ALL WISDOM WELCOME! But please, be gentle.

~~~~~~

Life After Hysterectomy

Musings:

Rich Businesswoman or Poor Starving Artist?

After my emergency hysterectomy, my needs changed. I met with my new counselor today. Our session was good. My new counselor has a PhD. in cognitive behavior therapy. She helps people, me, create new behaviors that support me to take care of myself while I heal from the surgery and the havoc the tumors caused. She is older and understands EVERYTHING about life after hysterectomy and what to expect as I heal.

She advised me to be soft with me.

She wants me to do 10 percent of everything I think I should be doing. :-) She gave me really practical advice: my sympathetic nervous system is in "freeze" mode because of all the recent losses. That's why I can't do basic things like find my keys or get out of bed or finish sentences. So she wants me to "baby" me: Eat soups, wear socks, put a scarf around my neck so I am not cold, etc. She says I need comfort. Safety. She wants me to nurture me while I heal.

It makes sense.

She recommends gentle yoga, even chair yoga, as well as using a timer to get up and walk outside every 90-minutes. I need to learn how to set and honor boundaries with myself instead of running myself ragged. I feel like an infant learning how to walk in regards to taking care of me, with love.

I am being with all the care I need.

It makes me wonder: How did I make it this far neglecting me so severely? I am realizing the reason I don't have a strong "yes" or "no" regarding me is that I had set my life up to be useful to others. I was so externally focused, I didn't see me slipping away. Now I actually have to talk out what I like and what I want. I bump into it... I bump into me.

My hormone doctor took my blood and has sent in orders for me. I have adjusted to Happy going to doggie daycare. I am getting better at being alone. Sitting still. Being silent. Resting. I am spending my time reflecting. Yes, I am CEO-ing but it's different now. I hired a Director of Opperations to run my company so I can heal without dropping things out.

I am letting the funnel go. A funnel is the series of opportunities for potential buyers to discover you, check you out, and eventually buy from you. It's the machine that gets leads (aka potential clients) to close sells. Without some sort of funnel, simple or complex, a business dies.

We started building this funnel in September 2018. Due to my divorce and my well-being, things were slow. If I am not clear, I can't write copy. I can't give direction, and I can't record a webinar so potential clients can see if they want to move forward or not. When I came back from cocooning in January, I was clear, and we started again with a great marketing agency to focus on paid traffic. I had also hired a resource to find, hire, and train a sales team for me, so I could have the surgery and not worry about my company. All of this felt good and right.

But then the breakdowns began.

We hired three salespeople, each an amazing woman, but at different levels. The most experienced one is still with us, but the other two are gone. I fired one and the other one left after her three-month training period was finished. And that's fair. We tried, and it didn't work. My new Director of Operations has a background in sales team management, as well as marketing, training, human resources, and business development. She is experienced at closing as well. So we lost two but gained a DOO. I'll take it.

Part of the breakdown with the sales team was getting leads. That's where the funnel comes in.

We had been trying to get this funnel to work for over six weeks. It was hellish. Facebook ads were rejected. Tech wouldn't work. Had to redo all the pages. Split-testing. Video production. Testimonials—all of it. My teams were working overtime, triple time, to troubleshoot, to strategize, to create new pages, subpages, redirects, and were directly emailing the people who opted-in but couldn't get through the application. And no one could fix it. Potential clients started to post on Facebook how they couldn't get through the page to register for their breakthrough session. I went back and forth with my tech and my ad team. The registration page worked for us—but not for some potential clients.

I let this go on for 10 days. Then I told my teams to turn the funnel off until the problem was solved. Within a week, my ad team retested and ran the webinar. The Facebook ads were disapproved and then approved. It looked like people could get to the registration page—which was a good guess considering we didn't run the reboot for more than a few days for them to apply. My ad team believed that the reason people weren't scheduling their calls is the webinar. And Facebook had started to reject our ads again.

The irony is that this same webinar converted in January and part of February. So his assessment was hard to hear. His recommendation was to come up with a new angle that didn't promise "quick and easy money" of any sort. That way Facebook would stop disapproving our ads. His recommendations come with a slew of unspoken requirements: new angel, new webinar, new copy, new opt-in page, new thank you page, new email strings, new follow-up emails, new videos, new Facebook ads, new budget for ad spend, new graphics, new order forms, new, new, new. Expense, expense, expense. And more downtime = no leads.

That's when I said fuck it.

I could feel the weight of wondering, trying, guessing, pouring onto my back. That's when I seriously considered throwing in the towel. Not as quitting but as giving up trying to save something that doesn't want to be saved. Surrendering to life instead of pouring good money after bad, pouring energy and team effort into a sinking ship, trying to make it work.

If I tell myself the truth, I see clearly that I spoke this. I manifested this.

I heard me saying, "I don't want this life anymore." And I meant it. When I say I was tired, that wasn't an exaggeration. I had hired teams that couldn't produce, lied about their skill set, or got angry and walked out, leaving me with a marketing mess to clean up and recover from. I never did.

Energetically, I can see the funnel is the past. It was born in survival. Forged in breakdown. The energetic in which something is created shapes the performance and life of that creation.

I created Defy Impossible, Inc. as a fuck-you to white privilege. My faculty voted against me for tenure because I wouldn't stay in my place, I didn't do things the "proper" way, and I didn't need them. I knew how to get my own money for projects. Stanford taught me that. I said my piece, which offended everyone (I didn't curse at the time, but it was still direct) and I wasn't focusing my attention on publishing in traditional academic journals.

My work was performative scholarship, and I published in popular magazines like *Glamour* and *Diversity Inc*. My scholarly performative work made the news, and I presented at the Sorbonne in Paris, at Harvard, MIT, Yale—but my peers didn't have a value for that sort of thing. So they expressed their disapproval with their votes. It hurt me deeply because I thought they were my friends.

White privilege had rendered me helpless one too many times. I refused to live with the effect of petty office politics in higher education and overt racism. No.

I became defiant.

When I started my business, I marketed to White Women by default (women entrepreneurs = white unless you specify another race), but they would only clap, cry, and buy the small packages—never the high-end ones.

I became defiant and marketed exclusively to Black Women. Black Men in the industry didn't want me on their stages. And White Men couldn't see how to monetize me with their audiences, so I wasn't invited in.

So I became defiant. I was committed to demonstrating we—Black Women—do not need ANY of them to make our own money. We can live on our own terms supporting each other. And we did.

Defy Impossible, Inc. has fulfilled its purpose. We won. I have, once again, defied the impossible. No different than getting off the streets.

No different than graduating from Stanford with a second master's degree and a Ph.D. I grossed over $5 million in less than 6 years with no government funding, loans, investors, or sales team—just me and a small loyal team that was committed to helping sisters get free from jobs, relationships, and situations that treated them like chattel.

As a cash-based business, all of the money goes back into the business to produce the next level of success. The benefit is, you answer to no one; the bad news is, you have to keep bringing in cash, ongoingly, in order to establish, sustain, and grow the business. It's a relentless machine. That's why funnels are so important. They provide the shot at bringing in the leads that eventually turn into cash.

At the level of Spirit, the reason the funnel isn't working is that it's fulfilled itself. I no longer have something to defy or fight against. Yes, I did all the right actions with the funnel, but in the wrong energetic. And nothing can move that way. As I let go of my former life, what also leaves is the defiance. One reason I feel so despondent is, I have won. The fight has left me; I no longer have anything to prove to anyone. Except myself.

Myself. Wow. It's a compound word:

my: (pronoun) 1. of or belonging to me (= the speaker or writer)

and

self: (noun) 1. a person's essential being that distinguishes them from others, especially considered as the object of introspection or reflexive action.

Ok.

So I am, in essence, an introspective and reflective action being who belongs to me only and exclusively.

Wow.

So I guess the real question is: What do I want for myself going forward?

I don't want to focus on money. Not because money is bad. But because in order to manifest money the way I do, one must heal. The magic elixir to manifesting is healing energetic wounds (personal, historical, cultural, familial, whichever still holds you in energetic, emotional, or economic bondage) at the level of consciousness.

Or, said another way, one must heal one's sense of "Self."

Most people don't believe that. They think if they do actions, they will manifest money. Money is manifested through energy, not effort. No amount of sweat equity, hustling, or working hard will produce millions. You can "make" money, but it takes healing to "manifest" millions. So no matter how much you do, it will not produce the desired outcome.

Trust me; I've tried.

It doesn't work like that, especially if you are a spiritual, conscious, transformed or faith-based person. Manifesting happens in the invisible. It's almost like God/Spirit/Universal Intelligence/Science/ The Great Creator /Energy desires something to come into material, tangible form and is looking for the right condition to move through to have that "something" show up. That's what I call manifesting.

Steve Jobs was the right condition for personal computers to show up in material form for the world. That was his destiny and he fulfilled it.

Rosa Parks was the right condition to make the Civil Rights Movement world news. She fulfilled her purpose on the planet.

Sojourner Truth was the right condition to speak up for White Women's right to vote. She gave voice to women's rights, human rights, and equal rights. She fulfilled her destiny.

So I guess God is, literally, getting everything that was in the way out of the way so I can fulfill my mine.

I can feel what is arising is to focus on manifesting all aspects of life, not just money. Manifesting my authentic life. I manifest from life's pain. I always have. The prayer I prayed when I was sitting on Monument Street, steeped in piss and beer, created or "attracted" Nanna to me. I have mastered manifesting. It's the reason I don't freak out (for the most part) when life sucker punches me in the gut.

My desire is to be an artist. A writer. I used to perform my writings. In cafes. At spoken word events. I produced, wrote, and performed a successful one-woman show off-Broadway. My poetry has won awards. So has my playwriting. I directed plays when I was a professor. I also taught. But neither of these fields was prosperous. The arts and education are the two LEAST lucrative industries. The benefit of both of these industries is time.

How could I be a millionaire as a poetic/performative artist? I have no idea. It doesn't seem possible. Or maybe I should be happy being an artist and making a decent living doing so. (CAUTION: #begentle Please don't question my faith. This musing is not a function of a lack of faith as much as a lack of vision.) I can not SEE how I can make money being a full-time artist. And I never have. I have always taught to supplement me when I was doing my creative work. I just never had the confidence that people would want me. My art, my words are me.

But that's the dream. Dreams need to be financed. As an entrepreneur/mentor/CEO, I am brilliant at what I do. Marketing. Sales. Content Creation. Service Delivery. Client care. Teaching. But none of those are me. Writing is me. Reading my writings is me. I am an artist and I don't know how to make that into an affluent career.

I am wondering if God took my funnel away because She wants me to focus my attention completely on truth-telling, healing, and manifesting… to let go of teaching a proven path to millions and focus solely on manifesting what a person REALLY wants. No, that's not it. To manifest their specific destiny is more accurate. And to manifest it from the truth of who they really are. I know how to teach and I know how to manifest in a systematic way rooted in one's lived experience. And I know I can do it.

But that's not art.

That's teaching. That's marketing. That's sales. That's service delivery. That's client care. That's chargebacks. That's late payments. That's default payments. That's merchant accounts. That's credit card fees. That's sponsorships. That's 50/50 rev-share. That's email after email after email. That's videos galore. That's reputation management. That's serving 24/7. That's hiring. That's firing. That's being stolen from. That's being lied to. That's investing in the latest hot industry trend that is geared for White Men. That's being used. That's being ostracized by your peers. That's being villainized by your market. That's being betrayed by the very people you tried to help. That's being lied on. That's being persecuted. That's being attacked to grow someone's platform. That's touring. That's up-sells. That's down-sells. That's side-sells. That's content, content, content. That's being on alert. That's living on social media. That's sleepless nights. That's missed meals. That's too tired to make love. That's gaining weight. That's so worried about the next launch you can't enjoy the success of the current one. That's being perpetually disappointed in yourself because you didn't hit your target. That's staying relevant. That's watching people who swear they love you steal your work, under the auspices of "inspiration" create an entire business out of it, and NEVER give you credit—or a percentage. That's people coming to your tour or event, or joining your list, or watching all of your lives and YouTube videos to try to copy your magic so they can monetize it on the hush.

That's business.

My point is this: I am tired. I don't want that life on any level anymore. I want a new life being my whole self. I don't want to be a business; I want to be an artist. But I don't want to be starving, struggling, or poor again either. I don't see how to be both at the same time. And even if I did, I wouldn't do my business the way I have done in the past. So which is it: rich businesswoman or poor starving artist?

It's a fucked-up choice.

Any wisdom? #begentle

4/8/19

Life After Hysterectomy
Baby

Everywhere I look, I see babies.
Or pregnant women.
Or toddlers.

I find me touching myself.
My breasts.
My hips.
My thighs.
My belly.

I notice myself wandering through the baby clothes section of Walmart touching onesies, pull-ups, tiny little baby shoes that fit in the palm of my hand.

And I cry.

I go to the maternity store to find baby lotion. I sneak a steal and gently press a dime-size teardrop-shaped of it in my hands. I rub my hands together, then cup my nose and mouth, so I smell baby.

I wonder…

…would I have been a "good" mom?
Kind?
Doting?
Patient?

What would it have felt like…

...to clean chubby cheeks stained with jam...
...to kiss a boo-boo to make the pain go away on a bruised knee...
...to pace the floor until there is a hole in the rug waiting for my baby (I don't care how old he/she is!) to come home.

I don't know.

I wonder if my child would have had my obsession for words and ideas...

...my zany humor
...my fierce loyalty.

Would I have handicapped my child by giving too much? Trying too hard to not be Momma?

Would my child have known the depth of my love? My devotion?

I have heard that there is NO greater love than that between a mother and her child.

I think this is true... even for the child who lives in the unborn.

~~~~~~~~~~~~~~~~~~~~~~~~~~~~~~~~~~~~

Hey Beautiful Baby,

You were never born.

But I want you to know I love you. I dream of you every night.
I see you in the twinkle of every little boy's eye getting into mischief.
I hear you in every little girl's sass when she doesn't agree.

I want you to know you are beautiful, smart, and special.

I didn't have you because I had to protect you from the world... from me.

I'm not a good mommy.

Bad things happened to Mommy, and I couldn't run the risk of doing bad things to you.

So I kept you safe.
I kept you safe in the space of The Unborn.

In my mind. My heart. The very air I breathe.

I see you every time I see a child with joy in his eyes.
I hear you in the belly-splitting laughter of every girl who expresses herself unafraid.

I hold you in my dreams, dear one.

I will never touch your baby soft skin...
...or nurse you...
...or bathe you...
...or change your diaper.

But that does not mean I don't love you.

I love you more than me.
I love you more than life.
I love you more than God.

I chose you over EVERYTHING.

I kept you safe.
I kept you warm.

And I nurture you.

Every day, when I tend to the little girl or little boy inside of every grown-up who thinks they come to me for business, but they really come for healing...

ALL the love I have for you...

...I pour into them.

I lavish my love of you on the baby inside of them.

I love you, little one. I love you so much. You are my baby.
My precious baby.
My pretty baby.
My baby love...

Venus Opal Reese (vor)

4/9/19

Life After Hysterectomy

Even

I have been bleeding.
Cramping.

Feeling like I still had my cycle.
Scared to say.
More afraid to find out if I have to have another surgery.

Nanna made me go...

I went to see my emergency hysterectomy doctor.
She said I am healing "unevenly." That's a notion.
Uneven healing. #wow

There are small abrasions in the space where my womb used to be that are causing the bleeding. She put medicine on them and scheduled me to come back next week to see how the medicine is working. If need be, she will apply some more, but she said not to worry. This is not uncommon. She encouraged me to take it even MORE easy than I have so we don't have to escalate to another surgery.

As I listened to her, I realized something that hadn't occurred for me before this doctor's visit. Especially taking into account the "unevenness" of my healing. I have been taking it easy—physically. I've stopped going to the gym; I am not lifting heavy things; I am eating well with room for cravings...

Where I have not been taking it easy is with stress.

I have PTSD and anxiety due to my past. It's appropriate. It would be naïve to think I could have come up off the streets with no trauma of some sort. Considering all the things that I could have due to my background, I gladly take these two. They are manageable.

The thing I need most in life to keep me balanced is certainty. Surprises fuck me up. I can do a yes or a no. Maybes drive me bananas. What's worse than maybes are open loops. Incomplete work.

Communication provides certainty for me. It helps me stay "even."

I fired my previous therapist and two-thirds of my creative team due to a lack of certainty. I kept asking for updates or information and couldn't get them. "Not knowing" and surprises trigger my PTSD and my anxiety, simultaneously. When I have to keep asking for certainty or imagining worst-case scenarios, I wake up drenched with sweat, heart racing, and panting from a panic attack. PTSD is real. So in order to get myself back to balance, I have to get certainty one way or the other.

I had another team member walk out on me.
Politely, of course.
Via email.
I called.
No pickup.
I responded to the email asking if things were ok and would that person, like to talk.
No response.
No communication for days. Nothing.
Not even "fuck-you-bitch-die-and-goodbye."
Just erasure at its finest.
I kept checking my email like a crazy person, waiting to get confirmation.
What I got was a polite goodbye and kiss my ass.

I now need to get the project completed, which is two weeks behind and beyond my expertise.

I must do this on my own or find another resource. And I will. But it brings stress to my body. #uneven #sympatheticnervoussystemshot

Each person knows I am healing, and they know about my triggers. But in their world, it doesn't matter. And it shouldn't. They—all of "them," not just this latest loss—are doing what is in their self-interest.

But that's not what evokes the stress. I respect their choice. It's the way they take away certainty by going out of communication that sends me into a spiral.

I am really getting crystal clear about how people lie in ways they don't think they do.

Leaving information out is lying.

Withholding one's self is lying.

Acting like things are "fine" when one's feelings are hurt is lying. If one is insulted for any reason at any level and operating on top of that is a lie.

I know. I have done all of them, especially when I was young in my emotional maturity and spiritual evolution. So I recognize the behavior.

Lies live in the dark, in the unsaid.

Withholding anything from anyone (be it a signature, a report, an update, a returned text, a pet, visitation rights, a child, a kiss, sex, money, acknowledgment—you name it) is a form of control.

It makes me chase you.
Follow up with you.
Think about you.
Worry about you.
Worry if I did something wrong.
It's pure domination under the auspices of being busy, avoiding confrontation, or procrastination.

I am realizing so clearly how many people who said they loved me didn't.

They loved me for who I was for them. Not me for who I am and my needs.

If I didn't say it right
or
had the gall to say where they dropped the ball
or
decline their request…

…they kept tally on the hush.
Instead of telling me or talking it through with me, they get busy or just leave.

Clearly, they had gotten all they could get from me, and I no longer served their needs. I am no longer useful to them. #ouch #oldwound #reopened #bleeding #uneven

I had become some sort of liability (i.e., money, time, attention, etc.).

Or they felt like I didn't appreciate all they had done for me.
Or I was too demanding because I wanted to know where things were in order to get something completed on time.
Or I was being disrespectful and had to be put in my place.

Or I needed to be reminded of how much I needed them or how important they are.
Or they have found bigger fish to fry.
And to be completely fair, I tolerated it.

(People didn't learn how to treat me by what I said.
They learned how to treat me based on what I tolerated from them.)

It wasn't the first time, Lord.
Deadlines were missed
or
I was left in the dark,
or
punished with silence.
Or attitude.
Or received a blame email.

In the past, I would call, text, or show up and insist on communicating until we got to the bottom of the breakdown. And it has cost me. It has cost me in every possible way, from money to well-being to peace and joy. Well, no more.

I quit.

I am no longer doing that.

If a person's heart is so closed or damaged that they take themselves away in any form instead of speaking the fuck up and staying in the conversation until we both get heard, there is NOTHING I can provide that will have their hearts stay open.

They want to be right or petty or punishing.

If you know, I am sick, weak, or in some sort of pain or distress, why kick me when I am down?
Where is the grace, Lord?
Where is mercy? The patience?
I have given it countless times to each of them.
But when I needed it, they show their asses?

It's cowardly, and it says a lot about a person's character.

They would NEVER say it out loud or even see their actions in this tainted light. It would go against their self-image. In fact, they would say I am making shit up. They really WERE busy. I believe them. I know they were.

But they could have called.

Anything would have worked.
Smoke signals.
Morse code.
A message in a bottle.
I would have taken ANYTHING.

Something, anything that would have acknowledged I am a human being and, just like them, I require care. I honored their needs; they didn't honor mine. So they leave it to me to get to the source of the breakdown. To work it out. To make it work. To pull it out of my ass. So then I have to follow-up when others are NOT communicating.

But when I do, they turn me into the enemy.

I get positioned as the bad guy.
The heavy.
The ungrateful.

The too demanding.
The too needy.
The *who do you think you are?*
The *how dare you.*

The *I don't need to take this from you.*
The *I was doing you a favor.*
The *you owe me.*
The *you don't pay me.*
The *you're done.*
The...

So I quit.

I am going to rest and take it easy as my doctor recommended.
This time I will focus on NOT doing things that turn into stress.

I am no longer checking emails. Too many surprises.
I am only talking to my Director of Operations, my Executive Assistant, and my private clients. I am going to tend to my peace of mind.
I am committed to healing evenly.

Prayerfully, when I go to the doctor next week, the medicine would have taken, and I will not have to go back to surgery.

It's good for me to get this lesson—to my BONES—now. I will not bring this behavior of chasing after people who vibrate at a lower frequency than me into the future, you, Lord, are manifesting through me, for me, as me.

Clarity is coming.

On the other side of this energetic pruning process in EVERY area of my life, my entire existence will be GLORIOUS beyond what I can see right now and anything I could have imagined.

I love you, Lord.
Thanks for hearing me out.
The hits aren't landing nearly as hard as they used to.
My reactions are shorter and less intense.
I can feel me not taking all the losses as losses.
It's starting to feel like pruning, shedding, a falling away of all that I thought I needed.
The more I heal, the less I need.

I look forward to healing evenly in all areas of my life, Lord.

Hope is arising.
And I am grateful.

Venus Opal Reese (vor)

4/16/19

Real & Raw Series

Joy

WARNING: SUBVERSIVE CHRISTIANITY BELOW.

If you're a devout Christian and have a traditional relationship with God, the Bible, Jesus, and the Holy Spirit—DO NOT READ THIS POST! It will offend you, insult you, piss you off, and/or make you want to start spewing Bible verses at me. Or it will compel you to defend your interpretation of the Bible. I have a personal relationship with God. It's a private thang and not up for discussion, debate, or correction/criticism.

I didn't meet God in the church; I met God in the streets. I met Jesus in the club. I am a street urchin with a foul mouth and a subversive imagination that is rooted in street culture, violence, and trauma. I was not built for the church. I was built for the marketplace. So please know, if you are holier than thou, I am not talking to you. I am talking to my people. My tribe. My "repeat offenders" who would never make it with your version of God. The folks who have eyes to see and ears to hear me: my tribe. We love the Lord, but we will never fit into your well-intentioned, yet judgmental, boxes.

It's important to note, I am an artist. Words are my medium in myriad forms. My work is inspired by God, no less holy than Saul turned Paul, the persecutor who wrote two-thirds of the New Testament after Jesus fulfilled the Law or any of the Old Testament prophets. So if you feel compelled to come for me, be warned. I talk back. In love.

Simply put: Don't fuck with me about how God and I roll. I clap back while honoring your Walk. My request is that you honor mine.

~~~~~~

I KNOW how important credit is.
It can get you access that cash NEVER could.

I called my mom, my sister, and my best friend.
Then I prayed.

"God, please, what should I do?"

And God said what God has been saying throughout this entire refine-by-fire season.

"Let. It. Go."

"The house, Lord?"

"No, Bae. The credit."

I could feel my hands grow cold and fire bubbling up in my belly, rising like bile in my throat, and then spewing from my mouth like hot volcanic lava.

"What the fuck, God? WHY do you keep doing this to me? I do EVERYTHING you say, and you keep fucking with me."

God laughs and indicates to Gabriel to pour him another cognac. He sniffs it with a smile, as he looks at me beneath the rim of his pearly white fedora.

Then God, being God, does some purely gangsta shit and says, "You asked for this. I am answering YOUR prayer. Remember?"

Humbled. And I do. "Yes, Lord. I remember. You are right. Forgive me. I didn't mean to come at you."

God laughs. "You are made in my image. You have a right to your temper. You got it honestly."

I love how he loves me. He is big enough to take responsibility for all of me and never punishes me for being just like him.

I smile.
God smiles.
When God smiles, all the angels in heaven hum in harmony and rainbows peek out from behind clouds. It's a beautiful thing when God smiles.

I sit at his feet and lay my head on God's lap. He strokes my hair with fingertips that feel like answered prayers.

"Bae, you are not your credit rating. No more than you are your feelings or your accomplishments. You are my Beloved, my wild child. You are not any of the things you have had. You are me. You are mine. And you are loved."

I start to weep.

"But God, I've made such a mess of the life you gave me…"

"Shhhhh—no, you haven't. Everything in your life has been my will. Including your good credit."

God lifts my tear-stained face up off his knee, and he looks me in my eyes. I fall into his eyes. I see oceans and mountains and ancestors swimming inside of Him. His eyes are alive with life.

His tenderness with me breaks my heart while he heals me.

"Your life is not a mess. I gave you this life because I needed you to understand my brokenhearted ones. They are yours to love. I made sure life broke your heart at every turn so your heart could hold and heal the heart of humanity."

God speaks to me in word pictures. I can see what he is saying, playing out in real-time right in front of my eyes.

"Just like Moses' life was designed to take those whining-ass-Israelites out of Egypt, and Jesus' life was designed for him to be crucified, you, Bae, your life was designed to experience pain AND stay pure of heart. Just like Jesus.

"So, no. You have not, nor could you ever, make a mess or do something wrong. I made you EXACTLY how I needed you made. You have a heart like David's, the Wisdom of Solomon, and you are as disruptive to the status quo as Jesus. You're my best creation. That's why you are my favorite."

I relax. I get it. God babies me, and EVERYONE in heaven knows it.

Happy, my puppy, comes over and looks at God petting me. He tilts his head to the left like he is trying to decide if he should be jealous or not. But before he can make up his mind, Gabriel, the Holy Spirit, and Jesus blow kisses at Happy that turn into butterflies and rabbits and birds.

Happy forgets about me and starts playing with these love offerings.

God continues to soothe me as he helps me understand who I am.

"Your prayer was to get everything that's in the way out of the way so you can fulfill your destiny. So I burnt everything to the ground. Just like I did Job. I took it all from you. Your marriage. Your Mercedes.

Your mansion. Your womb. Your friends. Your funnel. And now your credit."

God stopped petting me and spoke softly, his voice as hard, unyielding, and unforgiving as steel.

"Bae, I don't share. You know how jealous and possessive I am. So now it's just you and me. No other gods, remember."

I caught the steel. I heard him. But now God is having a flashback…

His fingertips grow warm like smoldering embers and coil in my hair. I know not to move. He gets like this when he feels threatened, disobeyed, or disrespected. "No god before me, behind me, or anywhere. You know the rules, Bae."

"Father, please," Jesus gently pleads on my behalf.

God looks at Jesus and softens. He can feel I understood, and his hands in my hair become kind again. Then he commands, "Get up. I did not make you to live your life on your knees. You have work to do."

I stand.

"Go do my work, Bae. The world needs you. I'm right here. I will never leave you. I love you too much. And if you need some help, reach for your brother. You really do need to stop punishing him for being the Messiah. It was a gender thing. Nothing personal. It wasn't favoritism; it was timing."

I give JC a side glance. I can feel the rage and resentment rising in my belly again toward God's only begotten. Then I suck my teeth.

"Fuck you, God."

God laughs. "Jealous. Jealous. Jealous. I hope you grow out of that. He is really quite effective."

I roll my eyes.

Jesus blows me a kiss that turns into a hundred blue jays and red robins that fly gently above my head in an upward spiral, singing. He glances to my right, and up from the ground, through the cement and streets paved with gold, grow honeysuckles and sweet magnolias.

I blush.
I cover my face.

God laughs, and the Holy Spirit comes and gives me a hug.

God says, "You see. Jesus wants your favor."

I look down at the floor and can see the glow of gold coming from beneath the concrete.

God drops his voice, so it rumbles softly in his chest like rolling thunder. "For me, Bae, will you please call on Jesus from time to time? He would love to support you. And besides, he understands your loneliness. He's been there. You let your sister, Holy Spirit, comfort you. If you would, Jesus can carry the weight of your Walk with you."

I feel embarrassed by my pettiness but stubborn about my position.

God is smiling at me with his eyes again.
The angels are humming.
I can see Jesus on his knees, praying for me to let him in.
Holy Spirit just hugs me more.

Happy keeps chasing after the rabbits and butterflies.

I sigh. I can't win here. I surrender. #kinda.

"Ok, God. I will forgive Jesus for incarnating as a male. I think it's some bullshit that because he fulfilled the law in the body of a fuckin' MALE, he gets all the hype! It's not fair, God—it's…"

God raises an eyebrow; the sun is eclipsed. He inhales, and there is a tsunami in Asia, a blizzard in Russia, and drought throughout the African continent all at the same time.

For the sake of the heavens and earth, I rush on. "I hear you, and I understand about the time periods. Jesus fit his time period to do this work as I do mine. I get it. Calm yourself. I'm not resisting you."

God sits back as Gabriel lights God's otherworldly Cuban cigar. The heavens and earth exhale.

"Now that that's settled - finish the forms, fuck your credit rating, and do my work. It's time."

So I listen to Joyce Meyer's series "The Character of God" and focus, praying without ceasing, on having the process be easy and effortless. What I couldn't get done in three months was completed in three hours.

God smiles at me and says, "Well done." He kisses my forehead, baptizing my third eye with his insight, as he holds my face in his hands.

And he says to me with the conviction and authority that a daughter can only get from her father, "You are my beloved in whom I am well pleased."

That's when I felt it.

In my heart chakra.
In the barren spots, that are my brokenness.
In my soul.

Like the butterflies Happy keeps chasing...

All the heaviness of the past disappeared.
I knew that the storm was over.
My Father had set me free from it all.

The angels busted out in a full-on hallelujah chorus; Gabriel poured God another shot of aged cognac.
Jesus wept. Happy tears. For me.
The Holy Spirit began dancing and speaking in tongues.

And Happy keeps playing with the butterflies.

I felt it fill me in a way no lover ever
could. I felt my heart flood...

brim...

overflow...

...with joy.

Venus Opal Reese (vor)

4/ 26/19

(First Try) My first attempt at screenwriting as a short film. Thanks, Sister Girl, for planting this seed. It's not formatted correctly, but it's a start. Let me know your thoughts.

Gentle feedback welcomed.

~~~~~~~~~~~~~~~~~~~~~~~~~~~~~~~~~~~~~~~

Real & Raw Series

War

Screen Short
By Venus Opal Reese

Setting:
Back alley. Streets of Baltimore. 1990s or present day. Either works. Rats and roaches clutter the trash dumpsters filled with garbage and broken trust. There's a brick wall at the end of the alley. One way in. One way out.

Character: J
J is sitting on a stack of milk crates, waiting. He is absolutely gorgeous. 6' 4" with long muscles like a basketball player in his prime. Flawless skin. Perfect pearly white teeth. Both men and women want to fuck J on GP alone.

J wears a black leather jacket, black turtleneck, black skull cap that rides low on his forehead. Black slacks and handmade Italian leather shoes. He rocks the purest, the most flawless diamond on his marriage finger that ever could exist.

J is perfect. He is charismatic. Seductive. Persuasive.

Character: Bae

Bae enters the alley coming up through the garbage in one of the huge dumpsters. Bae is stunning. The resemblance between her and J is striking. It's clear they have the same DNA. They both have impeccable bone structure, damn near identical body type. And they both exude power. But that's where the similarities end.

Bae is dressed in dirty rags that used to be white. Her hair is matted and tangled; it has not been combed since the day Bae was born. Bae has on a pair of steel-toed combat boots and packs a Glock. The streets have trained her well.

Her teeth are yellow, and a few are missing. Life has been hard on her. Bae is a street urchin who has been hardened by Life. Yet, Bae is still beautiful and can feel people's pain.
Bae sees J sitting on the milk crates like he's the second fucking coming. Bae starts to seethe silently.

J: What's good?
Bae: You tell me.
J: Right. I wanted to talk with you.
Bae: About what?
J: Us.
Bae: There is no us.
J: Yes, there is an us. It's time to clear the air.

(Bae is pissed.)
Bae: Here? You bring me back to the alley, the same street corner you left me to die on, to clear the fucking air?

(Bae is hot. Her rage is thick.)

J: *(Unflinching)* Yes, I did. We needed to —

Bae: *(Pulls the Glock and points it at his heart.)* Fuck you, nigga. "We" don't need to do shit. *(Bae cocks the gun and puts it on J's forehead. Bae talks through clenched teeth; her hand slightly trembles from rage.)* You left me here to die. Just like my father left Momma to take the fall for him. There's not shit you can say to me that will EVER make things right between us.

(J listens. Then he starts to bleed.)

J: Bae, I know why you hate me; that you blame me. For all the men who beat you, who ran trains on you. For the people who lied to you. Used you. Pimped you then left you. But you don't know the whole story. I have always been there, so has Pops you were never—

(Bae bitch-slaps him with the Glock. Bae bum-rushes him to the brick wall. Bae kicks him, pistol-whips him; tears stream down her face. He lets her.)

Bae: You said you loved me *(Bae kicks J in the stomach.)*, that you would never leave me or forsake me. But. You. LIED. *(Bae throws the Glock to the side and starts punching J.)* Where the hell were you when Momma put the gun in my mouth? Or when I was taking golden showers so I could eat? Where the fuck were you when I had my first blowjob at six? WHERE THE FUCK WERE YOU, J?

(Bae kicks and cries and kicks and cries and kicks and cries. J doesn't defend himself. He doesn't try to protect himself in any way. J lets her get it all out.)

Bae: You were supposed to love me. You can love any and everyone, but you couldn't love me. *(Bae stops moving. As quickly as her rage came, it leaves her. Bae looks away and just lets the tears fall…)*

(J is bleeding. He sits up against the brick wall. His eye is swollen. His lip busted. There is blood dripping from his nose. His mouth is starting to swell, but he doesn't care. He speaks softly, his voice thick with emotion.)

J: Give me your hand.
Bae: Fuck you.
J: Please. I know you are hurt and blame me. But please, Bae, all I ask of you is to give me your hand. You can kill me after. I won't fight you. Please Bae *(Bae looks at him with little girl, tortured eyes that have seen too much to go on faith.)*

(J continues.)

I'm so sorry I hurt you. You have every right to feel the way you feel about me. But Bae, please. I need you to just this once, please give me your hand. Then everything will make sense. I promise.

(Bae starts to weep angry tears. Bae hears his plea and remembers that beneath all the pain, Bae loves him. Bae slowly reaches out her hand to J. He takes it with bloody trembling fingers and puts her hand on his right side where he is bleeding.)

J: This wound right here, I took the knife for you so you could have a shot at having a life.

(He takes her hand and puts it in his hand. He puts her finger through the hole in it.)

J: This hole right here was put there as payment for you to have a voice—be it through writing or speaking or teaching. I paid for that with this hole.

(He takes her hand to his other hand and put her hand through that hole.)
J: This hole was the price I had to pay to get you off the streets.

(He takes both of her hands to his head and removes his cap. The scars are bleeding.)

J: They used barbed wire and electric shocks on my head so you could go to school all the way through graduating from Stanford.

(He is exhausted. His body hurts, and his mouth is swelling. He doesn't care. He keeps going.)

J: They used a power drill on my feet. They tied me down, put my feet on top of each other, and drilled through both at the same time. It hurt like hell. But better me than you, Bae. I felt every piece of pain in exchange for you not losing your mind and killing yourself.

I was with you, Bae, in spirit. I left you to protect you. I cut deals, slug bags for all the motherfuckers who run the streets, and I paid the price to keep you alive.

I was the one who jammed the gun when Momma put it in your mouth. I was the one who made sure Nanna went to work the day after you prayed to Pops to help you.

I was the one who took every hit you didn't receive. I have been your silent hitman. Everyone who fucked you over had to deal with me. Just like Pops taught us. I have righted every wrong ever done to you.

I was the one who paid for every favor, every act of mercy, grace, kindness—that was all me, Bae. I love you, Sis. I'm sorry you have felt thrown away. I died for—

(Bae stands up. Bae looks Jesus in the eyes.)

Bae: You didn't die for me. You died to do Daddy's dirty work. You can't play me, J. We come from the same father. I am as much his child as you are. So don't bring that messiah shit into this.

J. Fair. You're right; I didn't die for you. But I lived for you. I paved the way for you, Little Sis. Pops took out your stepdad Joseph because Father knew if he raised you, you would become the most lethal kingpin that ever lived. Instead, Pops put you on the streets to walk it out.

This is your season, Sis.

But you can't do God's work being pissed with me. So will you forgive me? Will you forgive me for failing you, for leaving you alone? I know they hurt you. I SO understand how cruel, malicious, and two-faced they can be. Will you forgive me for my sins?

(Bae looks at her older brother and drops to her knees. Bae says nothing. Bae just holds Jesus in her arms and rocks. Every place his bleeding hands touch, turns white. He puts both hands in her hair, and it unmats and untangles. It becomes thick, clean, and lush.)

(He touches her face and all the years of resentment and pain fall away like scales. Her skin becomes clean, and her teeth become whole and white as snow.)

(Her clothes turn into a pair of white leather pants, a white tank, white, red-bottom, thigh-high boots, and a white leather jacket with a hidden zipper that crosses her body. In her jacket pocket is a pair of badass Ray-Ban shades.)

(Each time Bae heals, a part of Jesus' body stops bleeding: his hands, head, his feet...)

(Jesus stands up, restored to his beautiful begotten self, and hugs his baby sister. Their battle is over.)

~~~~~~

(All of a sudden, the wind starts to whip up trash in the alleyway. Bae puts on her shades; J pulls his cap down to shield his eyes).

(A long white Cadillac comes to the opening of the alley and stops. The whitewall tires are embedded with real diamonds. #bigpimpin)

(The driver's door opens, and Gabriel steps out, looking like power.)

(He turns up his collar and walks around to open the passenger door. When he cracks the door open, blinding white light pours out of the Caddy as a white carpet rolls from the car door to the brick wall. Bae is on one side of it, J on the other.)

(We see the cane first.)

(It's an opalescent white stick with a mother of pearl handle in the shape of the Cross.)

(God the Father eases his way out of the Rolls. He takes his time, wearing a black-and-white pinstriped zoot suit and an all-white fedora and with a Cuban cigar held steady between his teeth.)

(He gets out of the car but leaves the door open.)

(Gabriel opens the other passenger door and Spirit steps out, looking like Southern Comfort. When Spirit shows up, life feels like a summer breeze, butterflies, and a warm hug simultaneously. Spirit is stunning in a 1920s flapper dress replete with a headband with a feather in it.)

God: Gabriel?

(Gabriel lights God the Father's cigar.)

God: I am glad to see my children have peace. This is good. Very good. Now get in the car. The human race is at war. Bae, you're up.

It's your time.

Venus Opal Reese (vor)

4/30/19

Real & Raw Series
Home

No one gets married to get divorced.
I know I didn't.

I fell in love with your kindness.
The bigness of your heart.
Your quiet compassion for my wounds.

Inherent in the divorce process is mistrust.
It makes sense.
When someone you love turns cold quickly, it calls into question everything before the cold came in.

I have PTSD.
I have anxiety disorders.
I am a dry alcoholic.
I am dyslexic.
I am a high-functioning autistic by some standards.
I am legally handicapped.

Getting out of bed each day is a victory.
I am socially awkward and have weak boundaries.
Surprises trigger me; the unknown causes asthma attacks.

Simply put: I am a hot mess on a good day.

As a child of the streets, I have survived by letting go.

While you were a kid learning how to play basketball at the neighborhood court, I was being trained to give blow- and hand jobs for money.

While you were playing spades and board games with your siblings or learning how to make cookies from your mom, I was being taught how to lie to the police and bust a green marble ashtray over a motherfucker's head while he was in a drunken sleep.

While you were a jock in high school and your classes were getting in the way of your social life, I was picking up the beer-stained crumpled one-dollar bills for the strippers to get a cut and sleeping in well-lit alleyways that had vents on the ground that blew warm air.

In my eyes, you were the American dream.
You were my one shot at "normal."

You were my stability.
You were my comfort.
You were "home."

I had never had a home.
Not in my entire life.
You gave that to me.

But...

...in every home, there is a basement.

And in the basement, way in the back, are boxes.
Old boxes.
With rusty locks.
Boxes wrapped in cast-iron chains.
Boxes filled with blood-red memories and violent, punishing behaviors, sadistic appetites covered with the sawdust of cruelty.

I brought my boxes into our home.

Boxes shackled in chains and deadbolts filled with pain, promises, and punishment too private, too dangerous to share.

My boxes sat in the basement of our love for 10 years.

Untouched. Undisturbed...

Until they were.

In one moment, all of my boxes caught fire, drawing nigh to each other, forming one box that fit together like a transformer, pulsing with red-hot heat, waking up a sleeping dragon.

The dragon had been cut into pieces, like Frankenstein's monster, and put in different boxes so as to NOT do what had been done to it. The chains and locks were false gods. The dragon was destined to wake, become whole and breathe fire.

As the dragon reassembled itself, it inhaled.

The chains and locks melted away like snowflakes on a child's tongue. And I realized neither you nor I were safe anymore.

The dragon stirred, dormant for 30 years. Waiting. Knowing that with the right provocation, accidental or intended—It. Would. Rise.

Violence.

Anger.
Rage.

Flew out of the mouth of the dragon, like ghosts from the past swirling overhead and started to burn the place I called home.

I couldn't stand it.
And I couldn't stop it.

I refused to destroy the only home I had ever known.

So I left.
I left home.
I left you.

Not because I didn't love you.
But because I did.

If you love somebody, you do NOT hurt them.
You take the hit. That's "law" where I come
from.

I wasn't willing to let the dragon, my dragon—me—destroy the only person I will ever love from a pure space.

I love you, precious.

I know our relationship is over.
I know my PTSD coping mechanism of letting go or going cold felt extreme and abrupt to you, especially considering you had only known my love.
I saw to it that you only felt the warmth of my love,
never the cold of my trauma.
I protected you from it... from me.

My protection felt like betrayal, abandonment, isolation, and disrespect to you.

I know. And I understand.

I can so clearly see why our divorce made no sense to you; that there had to be "something" in the shadows to make it, to make me, make sense to you.

But you don't have my boxes.

You don't have a fire-breathing dragon specifically trained to annihilate when threatened living in the boxes of the basement.

And nothing I could say or do would EVER make sense to your two-parent, middle-class-loving (by no means perfect) upbringing.

And that's why I loved you.

You gave me normal.
You gave me the American dream.
You gave me something I had wanted my whole life.

You gave me home.

And for 10 years, I knew what it felt like to come home from work and have the rich aroma of garlic and sautéed onions greet me at the door.

For 10 years, I knew what it felt like to hold hands, sit in silence at peace, and be safe.

For 10 years, I had homie/lover/wife/mom/boyfriend/girlfriend/confidante and lover all in you.

I used to love to hear you putter in the hallway, just walking from one room to the other. The sound of your footsteps and laughter as you talked with one of your siblings on the phone gave me comfort. It stabilized me.

You gave me home.

Our marriage was a glorious season in my life. I will cherish all the days of my life.

We won in our marriage. Very few couples can say that—divorced, shakin', or married.

No one gets married to get divorced.

The divorce process is inherently mistrusting.
I get it. And I understand.

I have no regret.
Beneath the accusations, misunderstandings, failed communication…

Beyond lawyer fees, court dates, and mediation…

When all is said and done…

When the dust settles, and the smoke clears…

I chose love.

Dissolving a marriage doesn't erase the love.

Love never leaves.

I choose to remember the love.

Thank you for giving me a home…
…I doubt if I will ever have one again.

Venus Opal Reese (vor)

5/9/19

Real & Raw Series
Guilt

Screenplay

Setting

Walking through a palace filled with world-class, beautiful paintings, sculptures from different time periods. A beautiful full-length mirror gilded in gold beckons at the end of the long hallway. GOD and BAE are talking. Gabriel is walking a few paces behind, standing guard. Jesus and the Holy Spirit explore the art pieces from different cultures and time periods. We can hear Happy barking from a distance, running around the palace. He's playing with Archangel Michael.

BAE
Writing?

GOD
Screenwriting actually.

BAE
Screenwriting?

GOD
Did I stutter?

BAE
Screenwriting?

GOD
Is that so hard to believe?

BAE
No, Lord, it actually fits... but it's NOT what I was imagining...

GOD
I know. That's why I sent it to you.

BAE
But GOD, who's going to produce it?

GOD
You will.

BAE
Me?

GOD
Yes.

BAE
But God, that takes MILLIONS!

GOD
So.

BAE
I can't with you right now... *(shaking her head)*

GOD
Bae, who's your daddy?

BAE
My god. *(completely outdone)*

GOD

Money is and has always been the easy part for you. *(Stops. Looks BAE in her eyes.)* What are you afraid of?

BAE

My tribe loves me and knows me. But the world? They are going to think I am crazy.

GOD

So?

BAE

Who's going to read my words, listen to my words?

GOD

Hundreds of thousands of people around the world already have. You're not telling me the truth, Bae. What are you afraid of?

BAE

What if the world rejects me? What if the world says "no," Lord? Then I will be disappointed and would have put my EVERYTHING into something that failed.

GOD

Rejected? Failure? That's your entire life. No, Bae, what are you really scared of?

BAE

I don't know, Lord.

GOD

I do.

BAE
What?

GOD
You're afraid the world will say yes. And see you. You're afraid of being attacked.

BAE
Yes, Lord, I am. There are so many people who feel like I own them or that I'm a freak or a liar. They will make up lies and come at me.

GOD
Yes, they will. That's why I put you on the streets.
So you can fight back.

(He looks at BAE and sees she is tormented by this.)

GOD
Beloved, hear me. You are right. They will come for you with lies and accusations. They will throw verbal knives and social media bricks at you. They will dig up old dirt to throw in your face, blacken your name, and attack your character to undermine your credibility. Old lovers, friends, family, colleges, peers, THEY WILL ALL COME FOR YOU.

(Looks ahead)
But that's when the street in you comes in. You were built for this. NO ONE IS SMARTER THAN YOU WHEN IT COMES TO TURNING PAIN INTO PURPOSE. No one can outthink or out-strategize you. You know how to fight. You are your father's daughter. And you know how to win.

BAE
Lord, I don't want to be like that. I have worked on myself for 30-plus years to NOT be like what I came from.

GOD
You need to give yourself permission to beat a bitch's ass, Bae. I need you to unleash the rage you have tattooed from your rib to your knee on the right side of your body.

(BAE looks away and starts to walk again.)

GOD
You are a savage, Bae. *(BAE stops.)*
My savage. You are only afraid to fight, to stand because you don't want to be like the streets. But you are THE BEST OF
THE STREETS, Bae.

(GOD drops his voice.)

You know how to win... Old Testament style...

BAE
But Lord, what if I hurt—

GOD
(Losing patience)
FUCK THEM, BAE! Didn't they hurt you? Are you a coward, some punk ass bitch who refuses to take a hit to keep the fucking peace? Bitch, please. Why do you act like their pain is more valuable than yours?

BAE
I don't, Lord. *(Sulky)*

(GOD grabs BAE by her hair and drags her down the hall to the gilded mirror. He forces her to look in the mirror. One hand is coiled in her hair; the other is around her throat.)

GOD
Look at you. Remember how they spread your legs *(He kicks her feet apart.)* and took turns?

(BAE sees the memory in the mirror. She tries to look away, but GOD will not let her.)

BAE
God, stop.

GOD
(Through clenched savage teeth) Look in the fuckin' mirror. Remember Momma sitting you in tubs of hot water and throwing it in your face with a saucepan? LOOK! See how your skin starts to cook in the tub. How many times did she make you take off your clothes and wait, knowing that when you sat there, worrying, waiting, you became so scared you would pee on yourself? You, a baby girl, sitting there naked waiting for her to put you in the tub. You didn't run; you are not a coward. You didn't fight her. You had more compassion for her than you did for your own scared little body.

BAE
(Tears up as she watches in the mirror her mother hurting her as a young girl.)

I remember...

GOD
(Takes a deep breath and pulls her close to him with his hand twisted in her hair and his hand still around her throat. He knows what he is going

to say next will hurt her. But if he doesn't say it, she will never get free. He loves her too much to let her keep hurting herself.)
Remember, you burned down the house in Fort Worth.

(BAE freezes. The memory shows itself in the mirror. She struggles. GOD has a lock on her body so she can't look or run away from her past, and she watches her eight-year-old self go under the bed with a lighter.)

BAE
That was an accident.

GOD
(Whispers in her ear. It's almost sensual.)
Was it?

(All hell breaks loose. BAE starts to fight GOD.)

BAE
Fuck you, God!

(BAE and GOD go at it. She stomps his foot, kicks his knee, goes for his balls. GOD shows no mercy. He fights back to take her out. She fights harder. They start breaking shit. The angels peek through the windows. Gabriel starts to interrupt, but Jesus shakes his head no. Their fighting causes natural disasters and starts to throw the solar system out of alignment. The Holy Spirit holds space. She creates an energy field around GOD and BAE to contain their fight, so it doesn't fuck up the universe.)

BAE
I didn't mean to kill the baby.
(Everything on every plane in the galaxy stops.)
It was an accident. I didn't realize the lighter would catch hold of the hanging material from the box springs under the bed.

I was looking for a jacks ball.
...She died in her crib on the third floor.
I watched them take the charred crib from the house.
It was my fault.
I didn't mean to... I

(BAE collapses in GOD's arms and sobs.)

BAE
I am so sorry. I didn't mean to hurt anyone... it's my fault...
it's all my fault...
I am such a fuck-up. I can't ever do anything right.
Momma was right. I don't deserve to live. I should be dead, God.
It should have been me, not the baby, Lord.
The baby... I killed the baby...

Why didn't you kill me, Lord? Why?
It should have been me... each time... it should have been me...

(GOD holds her. Jesus and the Holy Spirit come and stand nearby, holding space. The angels hum a memorial service song. Gabriel stands on the lookout protecting the space. Happy is somewhere nearby—in view—licking himself and listening.)

GOD
Bae, you have always blamed yourself for every bad thing that happened in your life. So you tried to be "good." But good has kept you in bondage. If you were good or good enough, you wouldn't feel guilty for the fire and for your cousin's death.

(GOD decides to share with her.)

You should know... she went quickly.
The smoke took her before the flames licked the crib.
She didn't suffer like you have suffered and punished yourself.

Look here...
(GOD directs her to look in the mirror.)

(There is a field of flowers filled with babies all in beautiful white cribs. Each has an angel tending to them. There are also toddlers playing in the grass and having a blast! We hear the pretty sounds that only babies can make. They are happy.)

GOD
We have a special place in heaven for the babies who come home to us three years and younger. Their innocence is gathered like magic dust and is sprinkled on the hearts of people to soften them. Because babies are pure love, they give their love freely to help others forgive.
Your cousin is right there *(GOD shows her a beautiful happy baby girl)* and her love is pure because you loved her. She knew. She knew you loved her and never blamed you.

(BAE has calmed down. She feels better.)

BAE
Thank you, Lord... What am I to do now?

GOD
Be bad. Stop being "good." It's just compensation for something that was destined. Your accidents are someone else's destiny, Bae. Without Judas, there would be no Jesus. Be imperfect. Hurt some folks. Stop protecting the world from you. Be yourself, Bae. Let them choose. You don't have to feel guilty anymore about being happy. Being alive. Everything is and always has been in Divine order, from the fire to the removal of your uterus to the end of your marriage.
It's time for you to fulfill your destiny.

BAE
But how?

GOD
Do whatever the fuck you want, how you want, wherever you want, when you want ,with whomever the fuck you want.
Fight for you. Stand for you. Speak up.
Talk back. Take up space. Say your peace. Be seen.
Burn bright. Go outside. LIVE! Let the world bow down.
And for those foolish enough to come for you...
Let. Them. Come.
You are covered by me.
I will not let you fall.

(The Holy Spirit stands in front of the mirror. She kisses it, and it turns into a door. She opens it onto a stage with a large theater, auditorium, stadium. The applause is so loud it sounds like happy thunder. It's an awards ceremony.)

(She comes over to BAE and gives her a deep, long kiss on the mouth. By the time the Holy Spirit finishes the kiss, BAE is wearing a red-carpet-ready evening gown.)

(Jesus hands her Happy and takes her hand. He escorts her to the door. She steps out on stage, and the room erupts into more thunderous applause. BAE looks back at her Holy Trinity and smiles. She walks up to the podium and hears the voiceover ☺)

Emmy winner for best new series... Dr. Venus Opal Reese.

(Lights out.)

Venus Opal Reese

5/16/19

Made in the USA
Middletown, DE
08 March 2021